The Thirteen Colonies

Connecticut

Books in the Thirteen Colonies series include:

12 102
$22

The Thirteen Colonies

Connecticut

Christina M. Girod

Lucent Books, Inc.
P.O. Box 289011, San Diego, California

On cover: *Landing of the Devries colony at Swaanendael, Lewews, Delaware, 1631*, by Stanley M. Arthurs

Library of Congress Cataloging-in-Publication Data

Girod, Christina M.
    Connecticut / by Christina M. Girod.
        p. cm. — (The thirteen colonies)
Includes bibliographical references (p.) and index.
    Summary: Discusses the history of Connecticut prior to its becoming a colony and after colonization. Describes life in the colony, its involvement in the American Revolutionary War, and post-war social, economic, and political changes.
    ISBN 1-56006-892-2 (hardback : alk. paper)
1. Connecticut—History—Colonial period, ca. 1600–1775—Juvenile literature. 2. Connecticut—History—1775–1865—Juvenile literature. [1. Connecticut—History—Colonial period, ca. 1600–1775. 2. Connecticut—History—1775–1865.] I. Title. II. Thirteen colonies (Lucent Books)
F97 . G53 2002
974.6 '02—dc21

2001001152

Contents

★ ★ ★ ★ ★ Foreword

The story of the thirteen English colonies that became the United States of America is one of startling diversity, conflict, and cultural evolution. Today, it is easy to assume that the colonists were of one mind when fighting for independence from England and afterwards when the national government was created. However, the American colonies had to overcome a vast reservoir of distrust rooted in the broad geographical, economic, and social differences that separated them. Even the size of the colonies contributed to the conflict; the smaller states feared domination by the larger ones.

These sectional differences stemmed from the colonies' earliest days. The northern colonies were more populous and their economies were more diverse, being based on both agriculture and manufacturing. The southern colonies, however, were dependent on agriculture—in most cases, the export of only one or two staple crops. These economic differences led to disagreements over things such as the trade embargo the Continental Congress imposed against England during the war. The southern colonies wanted their staple crops to be exempt from the embargo because their economies would have collapsed if they could not trade with England, which in some cases was the sole importer. A compromise was eventually made and the southern colonies were allowed to keep trading some exports.

In addition to clashing over economic issues, often the colonies did not see eye to eye on basic political philosophy. For example, Connecticut leaders held that education was the route to greater political liberty, believing that knowledgeable citizens would not allow themselves to be stripped of basic freedoms and rights. South Carolinians, on the other hand, thought that the protection of personal property and economic independence was the basic foundation of freedom. In light of such profound differences it is amazing that the colonies were able to unite in the fight for independence and then later under a strong national government.

Why, then, did the colonies unite? When the Revolutionary War began the colonies set aside their differences and banded together because they shared a common goal—gaining political freedom from what they considered a tyrannical monarchy—that could be more easily attained if they cooperated with each other. However, after the war ended, the states abandoned unity and once again pursued sectional interests, functioning as little nations in a weak confederacy. The congress of this confederacy, which was bound by the Articles of Confederation, had virtually no authority over the individual states. Much bickering ensued—the individual states refused to pay their war debts to the national government, the nation was sinking further into an economic depression, and there was nothing the national government could do. Political leaders realized that the nation was in jeopardy of falling apart. They were also aware that European nations such as England, France, and Spain were all watching the new country, ready to conquer it at the first opportunity. Thus the states came together at the Constitutional Convention in order to create a system of government that would be both strong enough to protect them from invasion and yet nonthreatening to state interests and individual liberties.

The Thirteen Colonies series affords the reader a thorough understanding of how the development of the individual colonies helped create the United States. The series examines the early history of each colony's geographical region, the founding and first years of each colony, daily life in the colonies, and each colony's role in the American Revolution. Emphasis is given to the political, economic, and social uniqueness of each colony. Both primary and secondary quotes enliven the text, and sidebars highlight personalities, legends, and personal stories. Each volume ends with a chapter on how the colony dealt with changes after the war and its role in developing the U.S. Constitution and the new nation. Together, the books in this series convey a remarkable story—how thirteen fiercely independent colonies came together in an unprecedented political experiment that not only succeeded, but endures to this day.

Introduction

Connecticut's Legacy

At first glance Connecticut's early history may seem to have little relevance to modern life in the United States. On the contrary, much of the legacy of Connecticut's first European settlers flavors American society today. The lessons these New England colonists learned about self-government, individual freedoms, and the need for unity continue to guide Americans today in many questions regarding political, social, and economic issues.

The first Europeans to dominate the Connecticut frontier, the English Puritans, established a way of life consistent with principles associated with Americans today. The tendency to view Americans as hard workers and thrifty spenders with a profound sense of independence and freedom is rooted in Puritan ideas, as historian Michael Kraus explains:

> Long after the Puritans ceased to be politically important, the well-known Puritan conscience lived on . . . to affect profoundly the American character. . . . They had an intense feeling about civic freedom, a deep moral earnestness and a horror of carefree gaeity. . . . Though the emphasis of

Puritanism was on salvation and morality it also was much concerned with industry and thrift.[1]

Moreover, although they did not practice religious tolerance, among themselves Puritans embraced certain liberties and rights that all Americans today consider their own. Americans can thank the Puritans for entrenching near-universal suffrage and the value of literacy and education as powerful tools against ignorance and oppression in our national consciousness. A New England Puritan minister's advice attests to this philosophy:

> The Education of Youth is a great Benefit and Service to the Publick. This is that which civilizes them . . . forms their minds to virtue, learns 'em to carry it with a Just Deference to Superiors . . . and by learning and knowing what it is to be under Government, they will know the better how to govern others with it comes their Turn.[2]

Puritans move into Connecticut. The religious principles of these early settlers continue to influence America today.

Although over time the Puritan religion changed and died out in its original form, its principles continued to develop in the later generations that inhabited colonial Connecticut. It is these colonists who helped figure out a way to build a framework of government that is strong enough to protect individual freedoms, and yet is organized in such a way that the individual can never be oppressed by it. This framework is the Constitution, which protects these rights and freedoms and allows Americans to live pretty much any way they please so long as their actions do not infringe upon the rights of others. Understanding how these rights came to be acknowledged and the experiences of the Connecticut colonists that eventually determined the "Supreme Law of the Land" is tantamount to understanding the value of the U.S. Constitution. This understanding is Connecticut's legacy to the modern United States.

Chapter One

Before the Colony

Before Connecticut became a colony the region was populated by native peoples. It gained attention from Europeans only when fur traders discovered the rich bounty along its rivers and when people from neighboring colonies began to flock to the Connecticut River valley in pursuit of greater freedom. It was the experiences of these colonists that determined the political direction Connecticut was to take after the initial period of exploration and settlement.

At the time of their first recorded visit to the Connecticut region, European explorers had been visiting the New World for nearly a century. In 1614 the Dutch explorer Adriaen Block sailed through Long Island Sound and navigated a river that came to be called the Connecticut, which was derived from its Pequot name *Quinnehtukqut*, meaning "beside the long tidal river." Although Block claimed the surrounding land for the Dutch, the Netherlands showed little interest in developing the region. It was almost two decades before the Dutch established a post to trade with the native peoples, which was erected at the "House of Good Hope," later to become the capital city of Hartford, in 1633.

At the same time another European group was vying for control of trade along the Connecticut River. John Oldham, an Englishman from Plymouth Colony, sailed up the river promoting English trade with the natives in 1633. When he returned to Massachusetts he spread word about the land to the south that offered good trading possibilities and a place where religious dissenters in Plymouth Colony might settle without opposition. Almost immediately the colony sent William Holmes to set up a trading post at the site of the future town of Windsor, claiming the land for Plymouth. In 1634 Oldham returned to the Connecticut River valley and established another English trading post at Wethersfield.

Dutch settlers trade goods with Native Americans. During the mid-1600s, the Dutch set up a trading post at what would become Hartford, Connecticut.

Puritans from Massachusetts migrated to Connecticut, settling around the Dutch trading posts.

Settlements of Puritans migrating from Massachusetts almost immediately swallowed up these trading posts, originally established to serve the economic needs of people in Plymouth Colony. Both Windsor and Wethersfield had become small towns by 1635. Moreover, English settlers increasingly surrounded the Dutch post at Good Hope, providing competition from English traders. As the English population grew, the settlers began learning to live with the native peoples of the region.

The First Inhabitants of Connecticut

The Connecticut region was home to about twenty thousand Algonquian-speaking Indians. They were members of small tribes like the Nipmuc, who lived peacefully in the northeast forests, and the Mattabesic, who inhabited the hills of western Connecticut.

There were also the more warlike and populous Pequot, who lived in southeastern Connecticut along the lower Connecticut River valley near the ocean. The Pequot had migrated from the upper Hudson River valley (in present-day New York state) around 1500. Researchers believe they went to the Connecticut River valley to escape domination by the newly formed Iroquois League.

The Pequot were not nomadic, however. They lived in permanent villages where they farmed, built homes, fished, and raised families. The Pequot subsisted on both agriculture and the natural abundance of the region. They raised crops of corn, beans, and squash, while meat from hunting provided the remainder of their diet. The men hunted large animals such as bear and deer as well as smaller fare like beaver. In addition, their proximity to the ocean made fish and seafood a large part of their diet.

The Pequot were not only farmers and hunters, but also fierce warriors. This highly organized, aggressive people quickly dominated the other tribes in the region, earning the hatred of those tribes. As a result, Pequot villages were heavily fortified from attacks by other tribes, especially the Narragansett (in Rhode Island). The Pequot used their reputation to monopolize intertribal trade, which kept the balance of power and wealth in their favor.

The Pequot, like many Indians, did not think of wealth in the same way that Europeans did. Possessions, like blankets or homes, did not have monetary value. Instead, Indians demonstrated their wealth by what they could give to others. The more possessions they had, the more they could share with others. Sharing wealth earned Indians great respect and increased their power.

This power was maintained by the Pequot through a strong central authority—unusual among most Indian tribes—which gave them a powerful military advantage over other peoples. This authority was exercised by a leader called a grand sachem who was aided by a tribal council. The sachem usually inherited the title from his father, but was subject to the approval of the council. Several subsachems were also distributed among the villages of the tribe. Subsachems served as decision-makers in their village and, along with the council, advised the grand sachem.

Although the grand sachem of the Pequot did not rule with absolute authority, his decisions were strongly adhered to by the Pequot people. As in other tribes, the council was free to disagree with the sachem, and anyone was free to follow his or her own course of action. However, there was tremendous pressure from within the tribe to stand together on any issue. Dissension could

---

Pequot Houses

Pequot villages consisted of longhouses (evidence of their former life north near the Iroquois) and wigwams, the more traditional type of house for the Connecticut River valley tribes. These houses were where the people slept and prepared and ate meals. Longhouses were rectangular structures made of elm bark measuring about 20 feet wide and 50 to 150 feet long. Wigwams were also made of elm bark, but were circular in shape. The frame was covered with animal skins or dried grass mats. In the center of the wigwam was the fire pit, and the surrounding walls were sometimes lined with benches. An individual family slept in a wigwam on the ground on furs or mats, feet facing the fire. Edward Winslow and William Bradford, in Mourt's Relation, *a journal quoted in Noel Rae's anthology* Witnessing America, *describe the typical wigwam:*

The houses were made with long young sapling trees, bended and both ends stuck into the ground. They were made round, like unto an arbor, and covered down to the floor with thick and well wrought mats, and the door was not over a yard high, made of a mat to open. The chimney was a wide open hole in the top, for which they had a mat to cover it close when they pleased. One might stand and go upright in them. In the midst of them were four little trunches [short wooden posts] knocked into the ground, and small sticks laid over, on which they hung their pots....

The houses were double matted, for as they were matted without, so were they within, with newer and fairer mats. In the houses we found wooden bowls, trays and dishes, earthen pots, handbaskets made of crabshells wrought together, also an English pail or bucket.... There was also two or three baskets full of parched acorns, pieces of fish, and a piece of a broiled herring.

weaken the tribe's political and military power and crumble its domination.

The Pequot Trade with the Dutch

When the first Europeans arrived in the Connecticut River valley, the Pequot stood undivided as the most formidable tribe in the region. After the Dutch arrived and built their post at Good Hope, the Pequot seized the opportunity to dominate trade with the newcomers. The Pequot routinely attacked the Nipmuc and Mattabesic to intimidate them and keep them from trading with the Dutch.

The Dutch were annoyed by the Pequot efforts to monopolize the trade; the Dutch wanted to trade with all the tribes in the valley. To force the Pequot to relinquish their control, the Dutch traders kidnapped Tatobem, a Pequot subsachem, and threatened to kill him unless the Pequot paid for his release and stopped attacking the other tribes. The Pequot offered a great deal of wampum (a highly prized gift of shell beads often strung on a narrow strip of deerskin) to the Dutch for Tatobem's release. Unfortunately the Dutch, who had never encountered wampum before, misunderstood its value and subsequently killed Tatobem. The enraged Pequot retaliated by attacking and burning the Dutch trading post.

This event played an important role in the future relations between the valley tribes and the Europeans. Despite the conflict at Good Hope, the Dutch and the Pequot both wanted the trade relationship to continue because it was mutually profitable. Consequently, the Dutch sent traders who could speak Algonquian to operate the post, and never again did they interfere with Pequot efforts to control trade in the valley. The Dutch also learned the value of wampum and were quick to use it as currency in the fur trade all along the eastern seaboard. For a while the Pequot and the Dutch prospered in peace.

However, when the English arrived in the region this profitable relationship was interrupted. The Nipmuc and the Mattabesic welcomed the newly established English trading posts, recognizing their chance to establish trade with this new group and form an alliance that might protect them from the Pequot. The Pequot did not appreciate this competition. In addition, they were threatened by the growing manufacture of wampum beads by the English, which increased the supply of wampum and consequently lowered its value. The Pequot, who made wampum by hand, could not keep up with the English, whose wampum was made in factories. The Pequot grew angry as their trade profits decreased.

Production of wampum beads in English factories threatened the Pequot tribe's handmade wampum bead trade.

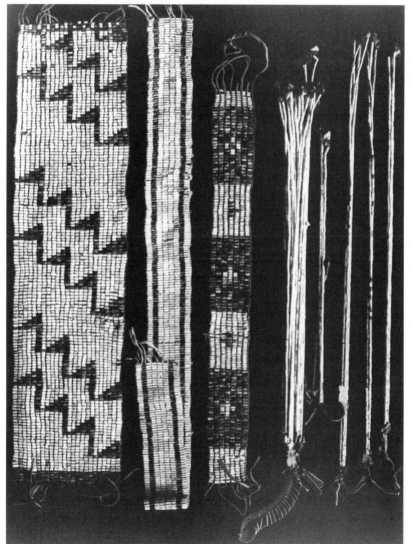

The Pequot-Mohegan Division

The Pequot disagreed about how to solve the problem of English competition. About half of the tribe thought the English should be attacked and eliminated, while the other half believed that the trade alliance should be shifted from the Dutch to the English. This disagreement might have been resolved had it not been for the personal rivalry between two former subsachems.

This rivalry had begun in 1631 when Sassacus had been chosen by the tribal council to be grand sachem over Uncas, his son-in-law. Uncas remained bitter and chose to oppose Sassacus on many trade issues. Sassacus favored continuing trade with the Dutch, so Uncas took the opportunity to lead the faction of Pequot who wanted to form a new alliance with the English. Their debates were heated and eventually became violent, with members of the two factions raiding either the Dutch or the English as they traded along the Connecticut River. By 1633 the hostility forced Uncas and his followers to leave the Pequot. They formed a new village on the river, near what is now Lyme, and adopted the new tribal name of Mohegan, which was the name for Uncas's wolf clan. The unity that had given the Pequot their strength was gone.

The Mohegan took advantage of this division by immediately allying themselves with the English and inciting attacks on the Pequot. Already more vulnerable to attacks because of the Mohegan split, the Pequot were even more weakened after smallpox broke out during the winters of 1633 and 1634, killing many tribal members. The Pequot continued to resist English expansion in the valley, however, despite these obstacles.

In 1634 the Pequot killed John Stone, a part-time pirate-trader from Boston who tried to capture Indian women and children as slaves at the mouth of the Connecticut River. Despite Stone's reputation as a cheat and a thief, Boston's Puritans were enraged by the incident and condemned the Pequot. Sassacus, the Pequot grand sachem, did not want a full-scale war, so he went to Boston hoping to ease tensions with the English. The talks failed, however, when the English demanded that Sassacus turn over Stone's killers, which he refused to do, and he returned home angrier than before.

To make matters worse, the Dutch had been effectively pushed out of the trade market in the valley in 1635 after the English built Fort Saybrook at the mouth of the Connecticut River. This blocked Dutch access to the river and forced them to close their trading post at Good Hope. With the departure of the Dutch, the Pequot were left with no allies they could count on against the English and the Mohegan. Small raids and attacks on trading parties further mounted tensions on both sides throughout 1635 and 1636.

In the summer of 1636 John Oldham, one of the original traders who had explored the Connecticut River valley, was killed by Pequot raiders, as William Bradford of Plymouth describes:

> John Oldham . . . went with a small vessel and . . . [went trading] into these south parts, and upon a quarrel between him and the Indians, was cut off by them . . . at . . . Block Island. This, with the former . . . death of Stone . . . moved them to set out some to take revenge and require satisfaction for these wrongs. But it was done . . . without their acquainting those of Connecticut . . . as they did little good, but their neighbors had more hurt done.[3]

As Bradford describes, this time the Puritans of Boston declared war on the Pequot and organized ninety men to march against them, without bothering to discuss their plans with the settlers of Connecticut. The Boston party traveled to Block Island off the coast near today's Connecticut–Rhode Island border, where they killed fourteen Indian men and burned the village and crops. They progressed to Fort Saybrook hoping to add more soldiers, intending to pillage villages farther up the river. When the Connecticut settlers learned what the Boston party had done, they knew they would be the ones to suffer the Pequot retaliation. Despite the settlers' disapproval of the actions, they provided the party with additional soldiers, believing the situation was beyond repair.

When the English had destroyed yet another village, the Pequot surrounded Fort Saybrook, killing anyone who ventured out of it. Then in April 1637 the Pequot attacked Wethersfield, killing six

Tensions between the Puritan settlers and the Pequot Indians erupted into a war that lasted more than one year.

men and three women. This was the first of several attacks that lasted for two months, taking a toll of thirty colonists. Finally in May the General Court at Hartford, Connecticut, officially declared war on the Pequot. An expedition of ninety English colonists led by Captain John Mason and seventy Mohegan warriors led by Uncas assembled at Hartford, intending to attack the Pequot's primary village on the coast (at present-day Mystic). However, when they arrived they discovered their army was badly outnumbered by the Pequot. Instead of landing, Mason chose to continue on to Rhode Island to add more recruits. The Pequot, seeing this, believed the English had given up, and sent their main body of warriors to raid the town of Hartford.

In the meantime, Mason entered Narragansett territory, and Uncas persuaded two hundred of their warriors to join their ranks. Now with four hundred men, Mason turned back toward the Pequot, intending to mount a surprise attack from the rear of the Pequot town. In his text, *The Wonder-Working Providence of Sions Savior in New England*, Edward Johnson describes the details of the attack:

The English . . . approached the fort. . . . The chief Leaders of the English made some little stand before they offered to enter [the fort], but yet boldly they rushed on, and found the passages guarded at each place with an Indian Bowman. . . . They soon let fly and wounded the foremost of the English in the shoulder. . . . They soon placed themselves round the Wigwams and . . . made their first shot with muzzle of their Muskets down to the ground, knowing the Indian manner is to lie on the ground to sleep, from which they being in this terrible manner awakened, unless it were such as were slain with the shot.

After this some of the English entered the Wigwams where they received some shot with their Arrows, yet catching up the firebrands they began to fire them. . . . The day now began to break . . . and now these women and children set up a terrible out-cry; the men were smitten down and slain as they came forth . . . there were some of these Indians, as is reported, whose bodies were not to be pierced by their sharp rapiers or swords . . . which made some of the Soldiers think the Devil was in them.[4]

In the end, the colonists set the fort on fire, trapping four hundred men, women, and children inside. They shot anyone who tried to escape, and those who did not burned to death. The destruction at Mystic broke the Pequot spirit. With their towns burned, their crops destroyed, their families murdered, and no allies to turn to, the remaining Pequot abandoned their villages and fled from the valley.

The English were not satisfied with breaking the Pequot spirit, however. They wanted to annihilate them, and more than anything they wanted to capture Sassacus. Sassacus had fled north to New York, hoping to gain refuge with the Mohawk, old enemies of the Pequot. Without even being allowed to speak in council, however, Sassacus and his warriors were killed by the Mohawk, who beheaded the grand sachem and sent their grisly prize to the colonists at Hartford in an act of loyalty toward the English. The

The Pequot and Mohegan: From 1638 to Today

The Pequot War officially ended in September 1638 with the signing of a peace treaty in Hartford. The surviving Pequot were dispersed in many directions. The 180 prisoners captured near Fairfield were forced to become slaves to their former enemies, with most going to the Mohegan and Narragansett. Of the 80 prisoners taken during other skirmishes, about thirty warriors were executed, while the women and children were sold to slave traders and shipped to Bermuda and the West Indies. The remainder of the population, about a thousand, was subjected to the control of the Mohegan and Uncas, making the Mohegan the strongest tribe in southern New England after 1644.

The Mohegan treated their former tribal members harshly, forbidding them to speak or even call themselves Pequot. By 1655 the situation was so dire that the English intervened, relocating the Pequot to their own reservations in eastern Connecticut. Although the separation from the Mohegan helped, the Pequot population declined until only sixty-six members remained in 1910.

Today one thousand Pequot members exist on the reservations, with a new sense of identity since being nationally recognized in 1983. They were one of the first tribes to open a gambling casino. As a result, since 1992 the Pequot have been the wealthiest tribe of North American Indians, echoing their former days as the most powerful tribe in the Connecticut River valley.

As for the Mohegan, they continued to support the English, helping them gain title to native lands and defeating the smaller tribes in the region so that Connecticut remained virtually free of native attacks thereafter. In spite of this loyalty, by 1774 all the Mohegan lands had been taken over by the government of Connecticut. Most tribal members migrated north, leaving only two hundred remaining in Connecticut. In the 1970s the Mohegan tribe was reorganized and received federal recognition in 1994. Today one thousand Mohegan are registered with the tribe.

remaining Pequot sachems surrendered and in September 1638 peace treaties were signed at Hartford. Of the three thousand Pequot alive when the war began, fewer than half survived. Those who did were sold into slavery or were incorporated into the Mohegan tribe.

The colonists viewed their victory over the Pequot as proof that God was on their side. One of the battle's leaders, John Underhill, asked, and then answered, "Should not Christians have more mercy and compassion? We had sufficient light from the word of God for our proceedings."[5] It seemed to fit their belief that Puritan settlement of the region was God's will. That was, after all, the very reason they had come to Connecticut.

The Puritan belief that God intended for them to establish a new society based on religious convictions motivated them to protect the freedoms that allowed them to build that society. Thus God's will became the will of the people. As a result the Puritans saw the necessity of developing laws and a form of government for the purpose of defending this "will of the people."

Chapter Two

Establishing the Colony for "The Will of the People"

After the defeat of the Pequot many more Puritans settled in the Connecticut River valley, bringing with them their ideas about self-government and freedom supported by the belief that they were fulfilling God's will. These settlers were seeking something other than excellent trade opportunities. They were, for the most part, seeking freedom to practice their religious beliefs as they saw fit. They quickly developed laws to protect their freedom in the new land. Their convictions about self-government never wavered, even when challenged by the English Crown.

The first challenge to these freedoms had occurred in the Plymouth and Massachusetts Bay Colonies, which had been founded as a haven for Puritans who sought freedom from oppression in England. However, once arrived, many Puritans discovered that they disagreed not only on the accepted practice of their faith, but also on how their colony should be governed. When one of the religious leaders could not agree on certain issues, he or she would leave the community and attempt to establish a new settlement somewhere else, taking several followers along.

Thomas Hooker

One of these Puritan dissenters was the Reverend Thomas Hooker. Pastor of the church at New Towne, near Boston, since his arrival from England in 1633, Hooker wanted to migrate to Connecticut because of political disagreements with the Massachusetts religious leaders. Hooker thought that the Puritan method of qualifying colonists to vote was in error. In Massachusetts only church members had the right to vote. Although most Puritans in Massachusetts followed church laws and practiced the accepted faith, only about 20 percent of the population were actually church members. Hooker believed that government should be placed in the hands of everyone who was subject to the laws, regardless of religious affiliation or rank.

Many disenfranchised colonists in Massachusetts agreed with Hooker's political ideas. Robert Child, one such colonist from the Bay Colony, expressed his frustration with the lack of popular representation in Massachusetts:

> There are many thousands in these plantations . . . freeborne, quiett [sic] and peaceable men, righteous in their dealings, forward with hand, heart and purse, to advance the publick good . . . who are debarred from all civil imployments (without any just cause that we know) not being permitted to bear the least office . . . no not so much as to have any vote in choosing magistrates, captains or other civill and military officers; notwithstanding they have here expended their youth, borne the burthen of the day . . . paid all assessments, taxes, rates.[6]

Some of the colonists who felt as Child did wanted to leave Massachusetts and settle where they could practice their beliefs and lifestyles without being restricted from the power to make political decisions.

Thomas Hooker and his congregation traveled more than 120 miles to reach Connecticut.

At first the Massachusetts leaders refused to allow anyone to leave the colony. However, eventually—although he was not able to convince the Massachusetts leaders of his conviction—Hooker was granted permission to lead a group of one hundred followers "whither they pleased, so [long] as they continue still under this government"[7] for the period of one year. After two weeks of traveling more than 120 miles, camping under trees at night, Hooker and his company arrived at the old Dutch Good Hope fort, which they renamed Hartford, Connecticut, in May 1636.

Soon Hooker began spreading his ideas that "in matters that concern the common good, a general counsel, chosen by all, to transact business which concerns all, I conceive most suitable to rule and most safe for the relief of the whole people."[8] When the one-year term was over, Hooker became the primary catalyst for uniting the towns along the Connecticut River valley, intending to form a new self-governing colony with a code of laws that was based on the will of the people.

Thomas Hooker's idea that "the foundation of all authority is laid . . . in the free consent of the people [who] set the bounds and limitations of the power"[9] was firmly entrenched in the Connecticut valley by the time the Pequot War ended in 1638. Now that the colonists could focus on political matters, the towns of Hartford, Wethersfield, and Windsor sought to unite under a government that reflected the will of the people. Immediately the three towns reorganized the General Court that convened at Hartford. This court comprised six magistrates and six deputies who presided over the political affairs of the three towns. Realizing they needed a more formal, stable government, however, after two years the court developed a new code of law, which later became a model for the American Constitution, embodying ideas of freedom and democracy that the colonists refused to relinquish for any reason.

The Fundamental Orders

By 1639 the Connecticut General Court, led by Thomas Hooker, had written up and approved a code of laws called the Fundamental Orders of Connecticut. This document served as the colony's constitution in the absence of a charter, an official document granting legal rights to a particular group (in this case a colony) issued by a governing body (the English Crown). It stated that freemen were to elect representative officials—including the governor—who presided over religious and civil matters. This idea about representation embodied in the Fundamental Orders made it the first democratic constitution in the Western world, as well as in America.

However, in actual practice, Connecticut was less democratic than the Fundamental Orders might suggest. A person had to be considered a freeman in order to have full voting rights and qualify for candidacy as an assembly representative or the governor. In order to become a freeman, a person had to be certified by a magistrate, and magistrates tended to certify only male landholding Puritan church members. This practice in effect limited the representation to only a certain religious affiliation and excluded women, servants, and the lower class.

Despite its limitations, the Fundamental Orders, a constitution that provided for popular representation, established the colony of Connecticut as an independently governed body with no allegiance to England. Rather, the people gave their allegiance to God. Hooker reflected this idea in a sermon supporting the adoption of the Fundamental Orders, stating "as God has given us liberty let us take it."[10]

Under the structure of the Connecticut government, the "admitted inhabitants" of the three towns—Hartford, Wethersfield, and Windsor—elected four representatives from each town every year to the General Court. The "admitted inhabitants" probably included other people in addition to freemen, and they had the right to vote in local affairs including the election of town officials. The more universal suffrage on the local level was due to such attitudes as that which a New England General Court magistrate expressed in 1635: "Particular towns have many things which concern only themselves [including choosing] their own particular officers, as constables, surveyors and the like."[11] However, only the freemen and the elected representatives annually elected a governor and six assistants who presided over the government of Connecticut Colony. The only other American colony that elected its own governor was Rhode Island; the others were chosen either by the British Crown or by the proprietor of the company who owned the colony.

Although the governor presided over matters of government, the real power lay in the General Court. The governor could not veto laws passed by the court, and he voted in lawmaking sessions only in the case of a tie. Moreover, the governor could serve no more than one term in succession. The requirements to be governor included serving one term as an assistant and being a member of an approved congregation.

While the Fundamental Orders may seem limited by modern standards, it was actually one of the most liberal codes of law in existence at the time. This was especially apparent when compared to the government of another independent colony that was being established at almost the same time just down the river from the three united towns of Connecticut.

The New Haven Colony

In 1638 a group of wealthy Puritans led by Reverend John Davenport settled at the mouth of the Quinnipiac River in southern Connecticut. These people embraced a lifestyle based very narrowly on the Bible and much stricter than those of the other Puritan colonies. Davenport had been the pastor of the Saint Stephens Church in London, where he had persuaded wealthy parishioner and merchant Theophilus Eaton to finance the migration of his Puritan con-

gregation to America.

After their arrival in Boston in 1637, where they spent the winter, Davenport's group decided to move on, believing that Massachusetts Bay Colony was much too lax in its religious and political practices. The group included many well-to-do merchants who chose their location, which was named New Haven, based on its accessibility to the trade market with New Amsterdam and Massachusetts Bay and the fur trade of

Reverend John Davenport led a group of strict Puritans to settle New Haven.

the Connecticut valley. One of the colonists stated that it was a "place fit to erect a Towne, which they built in very little time, with very faire houses, and compleat streets."[12] It was also isolated enough to allow them to follow their own principles of government and religion without outside interference.

These principles were drawn up in a document called the New Haven Fundamental Articles of 1639, which said, in part, that "the word of God shall be the only rule to be attended unto in ordering the affairs of government in this plantation."[13] As in most of the other colonies, only church members could vote and membership was limited to only a select few. The freemen of New Haven created a code of law that was based literally on the Bible. When traditional English politics conflicted with the Bible, the Bible was followed. This was evident by New Haven's dispersal of trial by jury because it was not part of biblical law.

Despite its strict code of law, New Haven continued to attract Puritans who desired, as they saw it, a more fundamental interpretation of God's will. The same year the Fundamental Articles were written, two more towns, Milford and Guilford, had been established. By 1643 New Haven had grown to include the towns of Stamford, Fairfield, Medford, Greenwich, and Branford.

Although similar in governmental structure to their neighbors along the Connecticut River, the New Haven colonists held a certain disdain for the inhabitants of the Connecticut Colony whom they considered morally lax. New Haven colonists defended their independent status with a militaristic attitude, and it was this intense desire to maintain self-rule that finally fueled the colony's decision to enter into a formal alliance with the very people for whom they had so little respect.

The New England Federation

Although both the Connecticut and New Haven colonists were secure in their belief in the right to independence and self-government, the dangers of life in colonial New England left them vulnerable to the forces of nature and threats from outsiders and the Indians. The Pequot War, which involved colonists from both

Connecticut and Massachusetts, made many in New England realize that they were stronger when united against a common enemy. In addition, they knew they could not count on help from England because the mother country had become mired in a civil war since 1640. Recognizing these realities, many New England colonists wanted to form an alliance with neighboring colonies in order to better defend themselves.

Connecticut's Role in King Philip's War

In 1675 the Wampanoag chief Metacomet, known as King Philip, incited by quarrels with the English over land sales, persuaded many small tribes from Maine to Connecticut to support him in wiping out the white settlers in New England. Although the fighting was limited to Massachusetts and Rhode Island soil, Connecticut militia and their allies—the Mohegan—helped turn the tide against Philip.

After an attack on Brookfield, Massachusetts, colonists in Connecticut became convinced that Philip intended to begin attacking the Connecticut River valley. As a result, two companies of Connecticut militia and Mohegan and Pequot warriors joined Massachusetts forces in scouting the countryside that surrounded towns and guarding supplies sent to the garrisons. The Connecticut forces were instrumental in repulsing Philip and his men at Northampton and Westfield throughout the winter because the Mohegan knew all the guerrilla tactics of other natives, with which the English were not familiar. In January 1676 the Mohegan and Connecticut troops pursued Philip's followers north, but they escaped when the colonial forces ran out of food and supplies. They were forced to march back to Boston in the bitter cold and later remembered this time as the "hungry march."

Nevertheless, the Mohegan and Connecticut men helped to find and scatter small bands of hostile natives, so that by the following summer Philip's cause had been nearly abandoned by the other tribes, and Philip himself had gone into exile. Soon after, an Indian informer found and killed Philip, ending the power of natives in New England.

Four New England colonies—Massachusetts Bay, Connecticut, Plymouth, and New Haven—banded together in 1643 under a "firme and perpetual League of Friendship and Amity for offense and defense, mutual advice and succour upon all just occasions, both for preserving and propagating the truth and liberties of the Gospel and for their own mutual safety and welfare."[14] The colonies called this union the New England Confederation, and it existed primarily for the purpose of defending the colonies against invasion by the French or the Dutch and the Indians, while preserving the separate governing bodies in each of the colonies.

Although the confederation was loose, it was not a weak union. Each of the four colonies was represented by two commissioners who formed a governing board. This board had the power to decide disputes between the colonies, divide the spoils of war, return escaped servants or prisoners who crossed colonial borders, and resolve issues with the Indians. The commissioners held the responsibility to "frame and establish agreements and orders in general cases of a civil nature wherein all the plantations [colonies] are interested."[15] Moreover, none of the four colonies could make war unless the action was approved by at least six of the commissioners. This particular covenant was directly attributed to the Connecticut colonists who wanted to prevent the type of incident that occurred when Massachusetts colonists attacked Indians in Connecticut territory after John Oldham was killed in 1636. While often fraught with tensions between the colonies, the confederation lasted forty years, and it provided a useful example of intercolonial cooperation that would later prove invaluable during the American Revolution.

The Connecticut Charter

While the Fundamental Orders provided an effective and stable government for Connecticut and the New England Confederation protected the colony from threats in America, the colonists had long realized that without a charter, they actually had no legal rights to the land they inhabited. They wanted the charter in order to secure the legal rights to landownership, but they did not want the charter to supersede the liberties expressed in the Fundamental Orders.

In 1662 John Winthrop Jr. (the son of Governor Winthrop of Massachusetts Bay Colony) traveled to London to secure a royal charter from the new king, Charles II. Winthrop brought with him a copy of the Fundamental Orders that the General Assembly of Connecticut wanted incorporated into the new charter. Not only was Winthrop successful in obtaining the charter, but he also managed to persuade Charles II to base it on the Fundamental Orders.

Britain's King Charles II allowed the Connecticut colonists to obtain a land charter based on the Fundamental Orders of the General Assembly.

Now, as a royal colony, Connecticut could solicit the military defense of England while receiving little interference from England in its governing affairs. The charter allowed the colonists to

> Take, possesse, acquire and purchase lands ... or any goods or Chattells, and the same to, Lease, Graunt [grant], ... Sell and dispose of, as other ... People of this our Realme of England. ... And Further, that the said Governour and Company, and their Successors shall and may for ever hereafter have a Comon Seale to serve and use for all Causes, matters, things and affaires, ... and the same Seale to alter, change, breake and make new from tyme to tyme att their wills and pleasures, as they shall thinke fitt. ... For the better ordering and manageing of the affaires and businesse of the said Company and their Successors, there shall be one Governour, one Deputy Governour and Twelve Assistants to bee from tyme to tyme Constituted [elected].[16]

The new charter not only granted all the land that comprised Windsor, Hartford, and Wethersfield, but it also included the territory of the separate colony of New Haven. At first New Haven rejected this inclusion, and struggled to maintain its independent status. However, in 1665 New Haven colonists agreed to become part of the colony of Connecticut.

For twenty-five years this royal charter remained in effect, and the colonists of Connecticut continued to govern themselves as they saw fit. However, in the 1680s the colonists were dealt the first challenge to their government with the succession of a new king to the English throne.

The Dominion of New England

In 1686 the new English king, James II, decided he wanted more control over the American colonies. He reorganized Massachusetts, Connecticut, New York, and New Jersey into a single colony and renamed it the Dominion of New England. He sent a new governor, Sir Edmund Andros, to America to enforce the laws of the new Dominion. Part of this enforcement included revoking the charters of the individual colonies. Andros ruled like a dictator, for he alone held the power to make laws, impose taxes, and administer justice. As a result, the colonies were no longer allowed to elect general assemblies.

Of all the colonies in the Dominion, none was more affected by these events than Connecticut. Although all the colonies had at least the right to elect the general assembly, most had their governors selected by the corporate proprietor or appointed by the king. Connecticut, however, had always elected

King James II seized control of the colonial governments in 1686.

When Governor Andros tried to seize Connecticut's colonial charter, Captain Joseph Wadsworth hid the charter in a hollow tree.

its own governor and was used to almost no control from outside the colony. Disregarding Connecticut's history of self-rule, in October 1687 Andros arrived in Hartford to seize the colonial charter.

The Connecticut General Assembly refused to hand over the charter, however, despite the threat of armed forces. During the heated debate between Andros and the assembly members the charter lay on the table between them. According to legend the room suddenly went dark. When the candles were relit the charter was gone. Captain Joseph Wadsworth was credited with smuggling the charter to the Wyllys property, where he hid it in a large hollow oak tree. It was in this tree, which became known as the Charter Oak, that the charter safely remained for two years.

Even though Andros failed to obtain the charter, he managed to take control of the government of Connecticut through force. During Andros's rule he violated several of the New England colonists' ideas of political liberties. He controlled colonial trade through English law, challenged colonial landownership, and tried the accused by maritime judges rather than by a jury. In addition, Andros angered the Puritans of New England by flaunting his

Church of England beliefs, including breaking the Sabbath by celebrating the anniversary of James II's coronation with fireworks. Andros's rule was sanctioned only as long as the king was in power, however.

The Great Awakening

In the 1740s a widespread religious revival known as the Great Awakening exploded in the American colonies. Much of it was a response to the dogmatic and ritualistic practices of traditional churches. One of the principal leaders of this movement in New England was Jonathan Edwards, a Yale graduate. Edwards was the pastor of a Congregationalist church in Massachusetts who traveled all through New England preaching and admonishing people to take joy in God's bounty and beauty, and to heed God's wrath if they failed to follow his rules.

One of Edwards's followers, John Davenport (also a Yale graduate), concentrated his preaching in Connecticut. He held public meetings where he admonished people to shed the vanities of life, calling for jewelry, elaborate garments, wigs, and other personal items to be thrown into a bonfire. Davenport's preaching was inconsistent with Puritan dogma and Connecticut laws regarding the established church. As a result, he was arrested and tried by the General Court. After being judged mentally disturbed he was sent home to Long Island.

Davenport's departure did not stop other evangelists from going among backwoods communities and preaching. These evangelists preached a mixture of rationalism and emotionalism that brought greater spirituality, practicality, and morality to those who embraced it. It appealed to the less privileged because it crossed class, economic, religious, geographic, and ethnic divisions. In effect, it created a church that was an original American, breaking with the traditional churches that maintained strong European ties. Connecticut leaders of the old Puritan elite were threatened by the popularity of these new evangelists. Citing colonial laws, they threw the evangelists in prison and recalled public officials who subscribed to such beliefs or attended the meetings.

The following year, 1688, the English Parliament enacted a bill of rights that gave Parliament more power than the monarchy and resulted in the removal of James II from the throne. This event, which became known as the Glorious Revolution, was followed in 1689 by a similar revolt in the colonies. In Boston, the nucleus of New England, colonists imprisoned Andros, saying "We have been quiet, hitherto, but now that the Lord has prospered [allowed] the undertaking [overthrow] of the Prince of Orange [James II], we think we should follow such an example. . . . We therefore, seize the vile persons who oppressed us."[17] This event officially ended the Dominion government.

With the end of the Dominion, Connecticut retrieved its charter from the Charter Oak and resumed its independent government. Although some colonies, like Massachusetts, were subject to changes that included some form of English control, for another eighty years the Connecticut charter remained in effect with little interference from the mother country. This allowed the people of Connecticut to go about their daily lives developing the unique political, social, and economic views that later contributed to the formation of a new nation.

Chapter Three

Daily Life in Connecticut Colony

The daily life of colonists in Connecticut was often difficult and full of disappointments; many people struggled just to survive. Farmwork was hard and required attention twenty-four hours a day, six days a week. (Sunday was the Sabbath and no work could be done except for necessities such as feeding the stock.) As Connecticut entered the eighteenth century, however, increasing numbers of people found work in the manufacturing industries, and the business of trade merchants was always profitable. Despite the work, colonists in Connecticut found time to participate in governmental affairs, found value in book learning and education, and followed the dictates of their religious faith. Education, economy, and government were all strongly influenced by the political and religious climate of life in Connecticut.

Government in Connecticut

In structure the government of Connecticut Colony resembled that of other New England colonies. Connecticut's general court had developed into a bicameral legislature, which meant that it had two sections, an upper and lower house. Freemen and admitted inhabitants could vote for representatives in the lower house, but only freemen could vote in upper house elections. However, many people in colonial Connecticut were more concerned with local issues that directly affected their economic status, and thus did not much concern themselves with issues of the central government in Hartford.

Requirements for voting privileges changed over time in colonial Connecticut but in general they depended on an individual's economic status and religious affiliation, and in most cases the person had to own land. Very few white colonists did not own their land, and thus most had the right to vote—at least on the local level. Although suffrage in the central government elections was limited to persons of high standing in the Puritan church, voting was extended to persons "of a quiet and peaceable behaviour and civil conversation"[18] in local elections, according to a Connecticut statute.

Despite the limitations, the opportunity that many citizens had to participate in self-government fostered a climate of entrepreneurship and self-reliance that fueled the colony's economy.

Work and the Colonial Economy in Connecticut

The people of Connecticut enjoyed a prosperous economy, in part because of the value they placed on hard work and self-reliance. These values were rooted in Puritan ethics, as one minister expressed: "Those who will not sweat on earth shall sweat in hell."[19] Although many people in Connecticut made their living as farmers, a large proportion of the colony's population worked as artisans or in manufacturing jobs, commerce, and the shipdocks. As the colony moved into the 1700s people began to move off the farms. Farms were difficult to cultivate because of the rocky soil, although the land was fertile in the valley.

Those who remained on the farms worked long hard hours, but the sales from their produce usually provided an ample living. Many farmers grew cash crops of rye, oats, peas, squash, and turnips and also cultivated apple orchards. Tobacco was also a profitable agricultural export. In Wethersfield the major crop

Connecticut farmers worked long hard hours to earn a living selling their produce.

became onions. Most farmers also planted a small crop of vegetables and grains for their own families' subsistence. Farmers also cared for a variety of livestock, including cattle, hogs, sheep, and chickens. The livestock provided milk, butter, eggs, and meat, and also served as sources of wool and leather for making garments and linens. Most farms were spread out over many acres, with their simple wooden frame houses separated from their neighbors by a mile or more. Farmers and their families were burdened with clearing trees and brush for their crops, building and maintaining their homes, tilling the soil, harvesting crops, and making household necessities. Moreover, they were constantly battling the forces of nature and the local Indians.

The difficulties of farming prompted increasing numbers of colonists to find work in the growing manufacturing economy of Connecticut. The town of Simsbury became known for its copper products. The brass industry exploded, with Connecticut-made brass buttons soon replacing those that were imported from England. New London was a large shipbuilding center. In 1740 Edward and William Pattison of Berlin, Connecticut, started making the first tinware in America, including plates, cups, saucers, and other goods. By the 1730s hats made in Connecticut were famous in England. In Salisbury and East Canaan furnaces and factories were built that produced iron goods. Ironworks became one of the largest and most successful industries in Connecticut, often prompting whole towns to spring up around the factories, which included housing for the employees, a company farm to feed the workers, stores, mills, and shops.

Some of these manufactured goods were collected by peddlers who traveled from house to house in the rural countryside selling their wares. These peddlers came to be called Yankees, a name that may have developed from the Dutch nickname "Jan Kees" (John Cheese) for English settlers in Connecticut. They carried with them in their wooden carts tinware, buttons, cloth, ribbon, pins, needles, toys, and other novelties that they often bartered with in place of a money payment for other kinds of goods. Yankee peddlers were

In this eighteenth-century engraving, a woman milks a cow outside a farm cottage.

well known for their business savvy. People joked that Yankees could even manage to sell a small piece of wood as nutmeg, which is a spice. (Connecticut eventually came to be called the "Nutmeg State.") English-born actor John Bernard described a typical encounter with a Yankee peddler in the late 1700s:

> [The peddler] begins by resting his pack upon . . . the door; its numerous contents [on] display. . . . Everything that is tried on seems to be made expressly for the wearer; she never looked so well in anything before. And equally strange is the discovery that, up to that moment, they had been living without a solitary convenience. Every one but the father perceives the necessity of Sally having a pair of shoes, Enoch a jack-knife, and the parlor a timepiece. . . . [He then] proceeds to another [house], and so on . . . till he arrives at the tavern, where he usually succeeds in trading the landlord out of bed and breakfast.[20]

The peddler was a valuable source of wares in the Connecticut countryside, but large-scale commerce took place in the cities.

New Haven and Hartford had been centers of commerce since their founding because they were located on rivers. By the mid-1600s Hartford had developed a large merchant warehouse district that exported horses, oxen, molasses, spices, and coffee in addition to food crops and manufactured goods. The manufacture of rum, made from molasses, was becoming one of the most prosperous exports in the colony by the mid-1700s. Rum was the major bartering product used to bring back gold, ivory, and slaves from Africa. New Haven had built a pier a third of a mile long out from its shallow harbor to deeper water. This pier served as a distribution point for smaller towns located on the shores of Connecticut and Long Island. Many farmers and manufacturers sent their goods to Hartford and New Haven hoping to sell them to merchants who would export them to Europe and the West Indies. These merchants were often the wealthiest families of the colony and they controlled the business of the vast majority of stores, merchant ships, warehouses, and maritime industries such as fishing and whaling.

Some colonists acquired a trade or profession either as a sole source of income or as a supplement. Those in the learned professions included lawyers, doctors, and ministers. Those in trades included carpenters, printers, blacksmiths, wheelwrights, cobblers, silversmiths, and many more. Often the head of the household ran the family business, making goods or providing services as needed, while the rest of the family took care of the farm or helped in the workshop. While there were many apprenticeships available for becoming a trade artisan, the education necessary to become a doctor, lawyer, or minister could be difficult to acquire in Connecticut.

Education in Colonial Connecticut

Education was highly valued in colonial Connecticut as a result of Puritan traditions. For the Puritans, the Bible was a literal truth, and every aspect of their society was based on biblical law. The ability to read was necessary to consult the Bible for all matters of law and morality, so parents were expected to teach their children

Some colonists made their living by performing a trade. Here, a blacksmith shoes a horse.

to read and write. However, many parents failed to adequately teach their children at home, leading the government to step in.

In 1650 the colony of Connecticut passed a general law requiring every town of fifty or more families to pay a teacher to instruct the town's children in reading and writing. The law read similar to this New England code:

> All Parents to teach their Children to read . . . and to acquaint their Families with the capital Laws, on Penalty of 20 shillings, and to catechise them once a Week.
>
> The Select Men may examine Children . . . and admonish Parents and Masters, if they find them ignorant, and with the consent of two Magistrates . . . put them into better Hands.[21]

Most of these schools were publicly funded. Local taxes paid for the construction of the school building and the teacher's salary. This allowed middle-class children whose parents could not afford private tutors or English boarding schools to obtain literacy and math skills. However, not all children in Connecticut had the opportunity to obtain formal schooling; many rural children lived too far away and could not travel to school because of dangers such as marauding Indians, wild animals, or inclement weather. These children were taught either at home or not at all.

Public schools varied greatly in their effectiveness from town to town, and some offered a broader curriculum than others. All Connecticut public schools taught reading, writing, and ciphering, which was solving simple arithmetic problems. Most also taught history, English grammar, and spelling while a few taught Latin and Greek. The best schools included studies in geography, higher mathematics such as geometry, and classical literature.

The colonial schools in Connecticut had few books and materials. Most schools had two books—a Bible and a primer, which included the alphabet, spelling words, and poems. Nearly all young children learned their letters and numbers from a hornbook, a sheet of paper attached to a paddle-shaped board and

Growing Up in Colonial Connecticut

Children growing up in colonial Connecticut spent a great deal of time learning how to be adults. They had chores and studies but little time for play. Parents were wary of spoiling their children and taught them that laziness was a sin. They wanted to raise children who were hardworking, respectful, and God-fearing.

Boys accompanied fathers on hunts, helped plant and harvest crops, and practiced the family trade. Farmers' sons who wanted to be artisans could become apprentices at the age of nine, when they would leave the family to live with a master for seven years and learn silversmithing, candlemaking, tailoring, or another trade.

Girls helped their mothers at home. They cleaned, cooked, tended the garden, looked after younger children, spun yarn and cloth, knitted, and sewed. Girls as young as four were given their first "sampler," a piece of fabric on which they embroidered the letters of the alphabet or verses.

Children had to follow strict rules for behavior. The School of Manners, an English behavior manual for children, was popular in the colonies. This excerpt is from Noel Rae's Witnessing America, *and provides a glimpse of these rules:*

[At home] Never sit in the presence of thy Parents without bidding [permission].... If thou must speak, be sure to whisper.... Bear with Meekness and Patience ... thy Parents Reproofs or Corrections, nay, though it should so happen that they be causeless or undeserved. [At table] Speak not at the Table.... Make not a noise with thy tongue, mouth, lips, or breath, either in eating or drinking. Stare not in the face of any one.... Stuff not thy mouth so as to fill thy Cheeks.... Smell not thy Meat, nor move it to thy Nose.... [With company] Stand not ... with thine hands in thy pockets, scratch not thy Head, wink not with thine Eyes.... Beware thou utter not any thing hard to be believed.

covered with clear horn for protection. Printed on the paper was the alphabet in capital and lowercase letters, numbers, short syllables that gave children practice with vowel-consonant combinations, and prayers.

In 1690 the first edition of the New England Primer was published and became required reading in Connecticut schools. This illustrated book combined the content of the hornbook with scripture passages and contained words, couplets (poems), and text for reading practice. The New England Primer was used in schools until the nineteenth century.

Children attended grammar schools, as they came to be called, through the "high school" years, unless they dropped out earlier, as many did. A few of the young men who completed their grammar school studies went on to higher education. In Connecticut, as in other American colonies, parents were loath to send their sons across the dangerous Atlantic to study in Europe, and as a result built their own colleges at home. Girls did not continue on to college because they were expected to be homemakers and mothers, pursuits for which higher education was deemed unnecessary.

In 1701 the Connecticut General Court authorized the establishment of a collegiate school for the purpose of training young men in theology and to become ministers of the Puritan faith. In 1717 it was relocated from Old Saybrook to New Haven, and named after its endower, Elihu Yale, who was the son of a wealthy Massachusetts merchant. Yale was only the third college to be founded in the colonies.

Most of the young men who attended Yale or other colonial colleges entered at the age of fourteen or fifteen. The major portion of the entrance examinations consisted of Latin and Greek. The college curriculum included arithmetic, geometry, physics, astronomy, ethics, politics, and theology. Most of those who graduated from Yale became lawyers, doctors, or ministers, and many went on to public service in political roles. Until the middle of the eighteenth century, however, Yale continued to be primarily a theological academy.

Yale University, the third oldest college in the United States, was founded in 1701, primarily to educate young men to become ministers.

Religion in Colonial Connecticut

The religious faith of the Puritans who founded Connecticut served as the basis for political, legal, educational, economic, and moral matters in their society. Although the importance and rigidity of this faith gradually diminished throughout the seventeenth and eighteenth centuries, the influence it exerted on Connecticut's society remained. From the time that Connecticut was settled until the early 1700s, Puritan doctrines dictated the life of most colonists.

Even as the authority of Puritanism began to decline in the mid-1700s, most colonists in Connecticut remained devout. They attended church for several hours every Sunday and often on Wednesdays. They adhered to the tradition of reading only the Bible on the Sabbath and did no work on this day. They abhorred immorality, laziness, and ignorance.

By the mid-1700s the Puritan religion had evolved into Congregationalism, and its adherents were no longer in complete control of the colonial governing body. Nor were they the sole managers of educational or community institutions. It became more common for such positions to be held by people from a variety of religious backgrounds, including Anglican, Presbyterian, Congregationalist, and Methodist. Catholics and Jews, however, were discriminated against in pre-revolutionary New England.

Although religious affiliation gradually ceased to be a requirement for holding political office, it continued to dictate the roles of men and women throughout the 1700s.

Everyday Roles of Men and Women in Colonial Connecticut

The roles of men and women in colonial Connecticut were dictated not only by religion, but also by the accepted social order of the time, which was heavily based on English traditions. Few people questioned these roles because they were too busy trying to just survive. Though different, the respective gender roles were important for maintaining life in the colonial wilderness and to some extent in colonial towns.

Women were the masters of the home and hearth. They planted and tended the garden, made candles and soap, sewed garments and linens, prepared and preserved foods, cooked, cleaned, and cared for their children. Married women had no legal rights to property or the family accounts and all women were excluded from voting rights. However, many women in Connecticut households

An eighteenth-century depiction of a Connecticut woman making candles in her yard. Married women's duties included soap making, caring for children, cooking, cleaning, and gardening.

A woman spins fabric on a spinning wheel. To make cloth, colonial women spun fabric from the wool of their own sheep.

could freely express their opinions to their husbands, and some husbands made a habit of consulting their wives in decisions affecting the household.

The lives of women in colonial Connecticut were filled with hardships. In the colonies people had to be self-sufficient, meaning that almost every article of use in the home had to be made by hand. Women spun thread and yarn from the wool sheared from their own sheep, as this New England writer attests in 1643: "They are making linens, fustians [strong cotton fabric], dimities [thin corded cotton fabric], and look immediately to woolens from their own sheep."[22] Then the thread or yarn was spun into cloth on a wooden loom. Finally the cloth could be cut into pieces for clothing, curtains, sheets, tablecloths, or blankets and quilts. The pieces were sewn together by hand using homespun threads.

Food preparation and cooking were daily chores that took up a great deal of women's time. They made sausage and headcheese and salted and smoked meats, churned butter and made cheese, pickled and preserved fruits and vegetables (which they gathered from the fields and woods or grew in the garden), and baked breads. Moreover, women were expected to cook at least three meals a day. Several dishes of meats, vegetables, fruits, dairy

Newspapers in Colonial Connecticut

Newspapers in colonial times were important because they were often the only way people learned about current events. The earliest colonial newspapers were little more than copies of British publications. Strict censorship laws in Connecticut limited the content of the papers to instructional essays, economic reports, gossip, advertisements, and poetry. Nothing could be printed criticizing the government. Very little attention was paid to intercolonial politics.

The focus of newspapers in Connecticut changed, however, after England passed the Stamp Act in 1765. Suddenly colonists had a vested interest in affairs outside their own community. Newspapers sprang up in many towns. The *Connecticut Courant* was established in 1764 by Thomas Green, a Hartford printer. Many papers did not last, but the *Courant*, which later became the *Hartford Courant*, survived and is today the oldest continuously published newspaper in the United States.

The most significant change was in the way papers influenced the activities of colonists. Debate over the conflict with England was a popular topic in post–Stamp Act colonial papers. Editorials became more common, persuading and encouraging colonists to unite against their common enemy, as did reports of legislative acts abroad and in the colonies.

Colonial newspapers continued to play a decisive role during the Revolutionary War. Determined to inform people of the war's progress, newspapers resorted to desperate means in order to continue printing. The *Courant* was a leading supporter of the colonial cause and enjoyed the largest circulation of any newspaper in the colonies during the war. Its fiery editorials were so persuasive that Tories burned down Hartford's paper mill to try to end its circulation. Undaunted, the *Courant* printed issues on wrapping paper until a new mill could be built.

products, and breads might be served for every meal each day depending on the wealth and stores of the household. In poorer homes women often cooked a single dish, such as hominy (dried hulled corn boiled till soft), beans, or a stew. Women in nearly every household made cornbread since corn was the staple crop in Connecticut.

Men were the primary providers of income and food for their families. They hunted, fished, cleared forests and fields, chopped wood, built houses and outbuildings, made furniture, planted and harvested crops, managed the family trade business and finances, and cared for the livestock. Men were also the defenders of their homes and communities, and most served in the local militia. Every man eighteen years and older received military training and was ready at a moment's notice to defend his community against invading foreigners or Indians.

As hunters, men provided the meat from deer (venison), hares, turkeys, ducks, and geese. They also caught fish and obtained shellfish such as clams, lobsters, and oysters. The men were also responsible for skinning and butchering the animals they hunted and the family's livestock.

Although in colonial Connecticut women were considered subordinate to men, their role as the center of the family unit was integral to New England's social order. This social order served as the continuing thread that held colonial society together in a challenging land. Men and women perceived their respective roles as a necessary partnership. These roles, however, would be stretched beyond traditional boundaries by the political upheaval of the late 1700s, as men left their homes to serve in government or the military, and women stayed behind to run the farms and businesses.

Chapter Four

Role in the Revolution

For more than a century and a half the colonists of Connecticut lived independently of England. They governed themselves, managed a prosperous and self-sufficient economy, and relied only on themselves for their defense. When England began to interfere in their business, the colonists resented the intrusion. Connecticut colonists were among the earliest supporters of a break from England and were eager participants in the war for independence. Although Connecticut was not a major battleground in the war, its contribution to the American Revolution can be measured in terms of the people who fought in the Continental Army, the men, women, and children who made personal sacrifices and contributions, and the abundance of supplies it contributed to the American military.

Seeds of Revolution in Connecticut

In the mid-1700s England began tightening its hold on the American colonies. The British Parliament passed laws that regulated colonial trade. It also imposed taxes following England's victory in the French and Indian War of 1756 to 1763 as a way to pay for the huge wartime debt. England thought that since it had expended a great amount of soldiers, artillery, and provisions for the defense of the colonial region, it was the colonies' responsibility to repay England.

In response the colonies reminded England that they had not asked for protection in the war. Moreover, accustomed to fighting their own wars, they had been willing to supply large numbers of troops. Over the course of the war nearly five thousand Connecticut men served as soldiers or scouts. Of all the colonies only Massachusetts and New York contributed close to this number of men.

Nevertheless, despite the colonists' protests, in 1764 England passed the Sugar Act for the purpose of "defraying the necessary expenses of defending, protecting, and securing the British colonies and plantations in America."[23] This act raised the taxes on refined sugars, made importation of foreign rum illegal, and heavily taxed textiles from France and Asia. Wines, coffee, and pimientos were also taxed unless they were shipped through England first. The Sugar Act angered citizens in coastal Connecticut because their economic prosperity depended on the sugar and rum trade. Many colonists refused to pay the taxes, using their charter as justification.

The colonists interpeted England's actions as violating their right to self-government as expressed in their charter. To protest this violation, the colonists bound together to refuse shipments of any taxed goods. Although the sudden drop in these commercial markets was felt in England, British officials responded by imposing yet more controls on the colonies. In 1765 England passed the Stamp Act, which required licenses, newspapers, and legal documents to bear a stamp that had to be purchased from the English government.

The public fury over the act was so strong that it prompted a group of radical Connecticut colonists to form a militant association called the Sons of Liberty. Soon citizens from other colonies, primarily Massachusetts and Rhode Island, joined the group. They stirred up public furor over the injustices of British rule by demonstrating in city streets, circulating anti-British literature, and inciting opposition. One member, the Reverend Stephen Johnson of Lyme, denounced the Stamp Act as a

Colonists burn stamps in protest of the Stamp Act, which required licenses, newspapers, and legal documents to bear a stamp purchased from the English government.

"dangerous lethargy that had lulled the judges to sleep and had taken strong hold of the Council."[24]

The Sons of Liberty encouraged Connecticut citizens to boycott the Stamp Act throughout the summer of 1765. People in Milford burned bundles of stamped documents in protest. In New London and Norwich the citizens declared Jared Ingersoll, the new stamp distributor, a traitor and hung him in effigy. In other towns, such as Lebanon, people tried and convicted Ingersoll's effigy, which was dragged through the streets and burned while crowds cheered.

In September 1765, the Sons of Liberty waylaid Ingersoll at Wethersfield. Surrounded by five hundred militant colonists, Ingersoll was forced to resign as stamp distributor or face imprisonment or death by hanging. In addition, Governor Thomas Fitch, who supported the Stamp Act, was denounced by the Sons of Liberty and ousted from office in the 1766 election, losing to William Pitkin.

The opposition to the Stamp Act in the colonies led to its repeal in 1766. However, the following year the act was replaced with the Townshend Acts, which taxed articles such as glass, lead, paint, tea, and paper. Colonists in Connecticut, along with those in other colonies, boycotted imports of these taxed goods and instead began to make these items at home and in local factories.

Although the Townshend Acts were eventually repealed in 1770, relations between the colonists and England were now beyond repair. The Sons of Liberty increasingly preyed on those who were loyal to England, known as "Loyalists" or "Tories." Individuals who were known to be Tories were often tarred and feathered and paraded through town. Their homes and property were frequently destroyed, and many were denied the right to practice their professions.

In 1773 England granted the nearly bankrupt East India Tea Company, a British enterprise, a virtual monopoly (meaning it was the only company allowed to do business in the colonies) on the colonial tea trade. This eliminated any competition from other trading companies that had previously sold tea in the New England ports. With no other company to do business, the colonists had no choice in the price they paid for tea. In response, colonists in Connecticut banded together with those from Massachusetts and other colonies in boycotting the tea market. The Sons of Liberty printed a circular that denounced anyone who allowed the East India tea to land in a colonial port.

Not all colonists in Connecticut supported the militant measures encouraged by the Sons of Liberty. Many merchants in New Haven and New London wanted to use more conciliatory methods to solve the tax issue. These conservatives supported the boycott but thought colonial representatives could negotiate a resolution with England. However, the conservatives, who lacked a united front, were outnumbered as the public became caught up in the militant furor.

Radical militants, organized by the Sons of Liberty, poured the tea of one Boston port ship into the harbor in December 1773 in what became known as the Boston Tea Party. England responded with the Boston Port Bill, passed in May 1774 as punishment. The

When Britain closed Boston's ports as punishment for the Boston Tea Party, depicted here, Connecticut and the other colonies quickly came to the city's aid.

The six-week session of the First Continental Congress, shown here in an eighteenth-century engraving, produced the Nonimportation and Nonconsumption Acts, which forced the colonies to boycott British goods.

Port Bill closed Boston Harbor until Massachusetts paid retribution for the destroyed tea. England thought it could starve Boston into submission. However, Connecticut, along with other colonies, came to the city's aid, sending an entire flock of sheep to Boston for the citizens' nourishment.

The harshness of the Port Bill prompted the colonists to call for a colonial congress. Connecticut selected three delegates to represent its citizens: Silas Deane, Roger Sherman, and Eliphalet Dyer, one of the founders of the Sons of Liberty. The three men traveled to Philadelphia where the First Continental Congress assembled on September 5, 1774. During their six weeks in session, the congress agreed to enact the Nonimportation and Nonconsumption Acts, which bound all the colonies in a joint boycott of all British goods.

All three Connecticut delegates supported the acts and encouraged compliance in Connecticut ports.

In Connecticut, while a small minority of conservatives protested the acts, most people supported them. They went back to making their own goods at home and in local factories and found substitutes for items that could not be duplicated, such as using native sassafras or sage in place of imported black tea.

When England responded to the boycotts by engaging in battle near Boston with colonial militia in April 1775, the Continental Congress reconvened on May 10 to determine the next course of action. Sherman was again chosen to represent Connecticut along with three new faces: Sam Huntington, Oliver Wolcott, and William Williams, Sherman's son-in-law. Before they had a chance to decide what to do, violence erupted in Canada. News came that Connecticut natives Ethan Allen of Litchfield and Benedict Arnold of Norwich

Ethan Allen captures the British Fort Ticonderoga. This offensive maneuver forced the Continental Congress to organize an army for war.

had stormed the British Fort Ticonderoga and succeeded in taking it. The congress had intended to keep a defensive force to fight back only if provoked by the British. However, Allen and Arnold's move, as an offensive maneuver, was inconsistent with this policy. If they were to take the offensive, they were going to need a real army to fight a full-scale war, and not just scattered bands of militia. Forced to act quickly, the congress organized a Continental Army with George Washington as commander in chief.

As hostilities commenced, Connecticut reorganized its colonial government, squeezing any Tories or Loyalists out of the system. Cutting off all ties to England, the General Court dismissed itself and then reassembled as a provisional government. Fortunately the colonial government of Connecticut had been made up largely of Patriots, who were retained in office in the provisional government. The conflict between Patriots and Tories was stronger in other colonies that had royal governors and had been subject to less control over their own affairs. In these colonies Tories had more authority and influence. In fact, Connecticut was the only colony that retained its pre-revolutionary governor, the radical Jonathan Trumbull. With the public in Connecticut so eager to denounce England and its supporters, Trumbull enjoyed immense support throughout the colony. He was, however, undecided about how to deal with Tories in his colony.

General George Washington, a friend of Trumbull's, helped the governor sort out the Tory issue. Washington advised Trumbull, "Why should persons who are preying upon the vitals of their country be suffered to stalk at large, whilst we know they will do us every mischief in their power?"[25] Trumbull took this as a promise of military protection from Washington's army and decided to take action against the Tories. Thus Connecticut became the first colony to pass laws against the Tories. The laws defined treason and were designed to promote loyalty to the American cause.

As the fighting continued, the delegates of the Continental Congress, who remained in session for the entire duration of the war (seven years), maintained a fighting army, kept the colonies united, and negotiated wartime aid with the heads of foreign states.

Before all this could happen, however, the delegates realized they had to form their own entity that could be recognized as separate and sovereign by other nations. Therefore, the members of the Continental Congress secretly selected five men to draft a document declaring the colonies to be a body of united states separate from the jurisdiction and authority of England. Roger Sherman of Connecticut was chosen along with Thomas Jefferson, John Adams, Benjamin Franklin, and Robert R. Livingston to create this decisive document. As a committee the men worked together for three weeks, bringing the finished work before the congress for approval on July 1, 1776. When the Declaration of Independence was formally adopted on July 4, 1776, Connecticut governor Jonathan Trumbull wholeheartedly supported it and urged his colony's citizens to do the same. Connecticut's citizens soon showed their support of the fight for independence as the war, now called a revolution, progressed.

The War in Connecticut

After the first gunfire between British troops and colonial militia had been exchanged in Massachusetts at Lexington and Concord, riders had galloped throughout the Connecticut countryside

The Continental Congress adopts the Declaration of Independence on July 4, 1776. Roger Sherman of Connecticut was one of five men chosen to draft the revolutionary document.

alerting people to the hostilities. It did not take long for Connecticut citizens to respond to the news. Within a few days thirty-six hundred militiamen had gathered and begun to march north to Boston where they intended to join a larger armed force. One soldier who answered the call to arms wrote a letter describing the huge response to the Patriot cause in Connecticut:

> We are all in motion here ... one hundred young men, who cheerfully offered their service, twenty days provision and sixty-four rounds per man. They are all well armed and in high spirits. My brother has gone with them and others. ... Our neighboring towns are all arming and moving. Men of the first character shoulder their arms and march off for the field of action. We should by night have several thousands from this Colony on their march. ... We fix on our standards and drums the Colony arms, with the motto ... round it in letters of gold, which we construe thus: "God, who transplanted us hither, will support us."[26]

Throughout the revolution many Connecticut citizens sacrificed their lives and fortunes for the sake of the ideals of freedom. In all about forty thousand men from Connecticut served in the Continental Army. Some of these people became folk heroes, like Ethan Allen, who had stormed Fort Ticonderoga, and Nathan Hale, who was hung by the British as a spy.

In addition to soldiers, Connecticut contributed a major portion of provisions to Washington's army. All over the colony factories sprang up to manufacture cannons, munitions, guns, and powder. By 1775 the first gunpowder mill in the colony was operating in Hartford. Local citizens took lead from their rooftops and windows (where lead had been used as weights) and melted it down so factories could fashion it into bullets and cannonballs. Many warships were constructed in the port of New Haven, which had formerly bustled with merchant ships.

The principal force behind the steady production of army supplies was Governor Trumbull, who served in office during the entire war. From his office he developed a successful system for distributing supplies to the army. Trumbull intervened during the winter of 1778 when Washington's troops were starving in the freezing weather at Valley Forge, Pennsylvania. Trumbull arranged for several herds of cattle to be driven in the snow from Hartford to Pennsylvania, an act that greatly helped the floundering troops survive.

In addition to providing supplies, Connecticut played a large role in preying upon British supply ships in the ocean. New London in particular was the homeport for several privately owned armed

The Truth about Nathan Hale

Nathan Hale was born on June 6, 1755, in Coventry, Connecticut, where he grew up on a prosperous 240-acre farm. A Yale graduate, he worked for two years as a schoolmaster. When war broke out he resigned to join George Washington's army.

Hale served for a year without seeing much action. When Washington sought a volunteer for a spy mission, Hale immediately jumped at the opportunity to do something important for the colonial cause.

Hale relayed the news to his friend, Captain William Hull, who recorded their conversation in an 1848 memoir. George DeWan relates an excerpt from this memoir in his *Long Island Historical Journal* article "Nathan Hale: Failed Spy, Superb Patriot."

> [He was] too frank and open for deceit and disguise . . . I ended by saying that should he undertake the enterprise, his short, bright career, would close with an ignominious death. "I am fully sensible of the consequences of discovery and capture in such a situation," Hale responded. "But for a year I have been attached to the army, and have not rendered any material service. . . . I will reflect, and do nothing but what duty demands."

Hull's fears proved to be justified. On September 21, 1776, the British captured and questioned Hale. He admitted he had been on a spy mission for Washington. He was ordered hanged at eleven o'clock the next morning, ships, which the Connecticut government licensed to attack enemy vessels. The supplies that were seized from these ships were then taken back to New London where they were stored in warehouses until they could be distributed to colonial troops.

Two factors made Connecticut a target of enemy reprisal: its manufacturing centers and its reputation for attacking British ships. In 1777 the British raided the town of Danbury and burned its warehouses full of munitions and supplies intended for the Continental Army. Two years later, in February 1779, the British attempted to destroy a saltworks at Greenwich, but

---

after which his body was left suspended for three days. He was finally cut down and thrown in an unmarked grave on Manhattan Island.

Historians do not agree on what exactly Hale's famous last words were. In 1777 a newspaper reported that Hale had said, "if he had ten thousand lives, he would lay them all down, if called to it, in defence of his injured, bleeding country." Another article quoted him as saying, "my only regret is, that I have not more lives than one to offer in its service." The more commonly used quote of "I only regret that I have but one life to lose for my country," is derived from Hull's memoir.

British troops prepare to hang Patriot Nathan Hale for spying.

Governor Trumbull's office in Lebanon, Connecticut, served as a key center for supply distribution during the war.

General Israel Putnam was successful in driving them off. Later that same year British forces marched through Fairfield and Norwalk, burning and looting the towns. New Haven was also attacked but escaped destruction, even though as a shipbuilding center it was strategically important. The bloodiest battle fought on Connecticut soil, however, occurred near the end of the war near New London.

By 1781 New London had succeeded in increasing its privateer loot every year, with its richest haul taken from the British ship *Hannah* that summer. The *Hannah*'s cargo included personal items belonging to British officers who were currently occupying New York City. This precious cargo was added to the wealth bulging from New London's warehouses. The city's wealth was not well protected, however.

Since the beginning of the war Connecticut's government had voiced concerns about New London's vulnerability to attack. Money was scarce, however, and the building of Fort Trumbull, intended for the town's protection, remained incomplete by 1781. In spite of this the community felt safe with the defense of the finished Fort Griswold, which protected the harbor, nearby across the Thames River.

Despite the presence of Fort Griswold, British authorities were aware that the warehouses in the city across the river were not well fortified. Looking for a convenient way to distract Washington and his army, who were moving swiftly south, and chafing from the loss of the personal possessions in the *Hannah*, the British decided to mount an attack on New London. They put Benedict Arnold, who had defected from the American cause the previous year after arguing with colonial military officials, in command of the attack. Arnold, who was a native of the neighboring town of Norwich, knew the harbor and surrounding area well.

On the morning of September 6, 1781, Arnold led his company of eight hundred men into New London, where the townspeople awoke and fled without offering any resistance. The British troops set the enormous warehouses on fire and burned the ships and wharves in the harbor. Almost the entire town—143 buildings—was burned.

On the other side of the river, Arnold's cocommander led another eight hundred British soldiers through the nearby swamps and woods toward Fort Griswold. That morning the fort was garrisoned with 150 militiamen under the command of Colonel William Ledyard.

American Benedict Arnold, pictured here in a nineteenth-century etching, defected to the British cause and led attacks on New London and Fort Griswold.

Although grossly outnumbered, Ledyard decided he and his men would defend the fort because he was expecting reinforcements at any moment. This account, given by the historical society preserving Fort Griswold today, records the events that followed:

> Colonel Eyre [the British commander] . . . sent forward a flag demanding surrender. Ledyard refused. The demand was made again and Eyre threatened that if they were forced to storm the fort, no quarter would be given to its defenders. The response was the same.
>
> The British force immediately spread their ranks and advanced on Fort Griswold. As they neared the ditch [surrounding the fort], they were met by an artillery barrage that killed and wounded many, but the seasoned and disciplined troops continued their charge. Some tried to gain the southwest bastion but they were repulsed and Colonel Eyre was badly wounded. Under heavy musket fire, another group dislodged some pickets and by hand to hand combat reached a cannon and turned it against the garrison. Another party led by [British] Major Montgomery charged with fixed bayonets. They were met with long spears and the major was killed. A few of the regulars managed to reach the gate and open it and the enemy force marched in. . . . Seeing this Colonel Ledyard ordered his men to stop fighting, but some action continued on both sides.
>
> . . . after Ledyard gave up his sword in surrender he was immediately killed with it and . . . a massacre ensued. Before the "massacre" it is claimed that less than ten Americans had been killed, but when it was over, more than eighty of the garrison lay dead and mutilated and more than half of the remainder were severely wounded.[27]

The defeats at New London and Fort Griswold were devastating to the citizens of Connecticut, especially because they had been orchestrated by Arnold, one of their own natives. But in spite of the destruction, by the time of the attack the British were already nearly

Newgate Prison

During the Revolutionary War the colonial forces imprisoned hundreds of British soldiers in what became known to the English as the infamous Newgate Prison. It was actually an abandoned copper mine located near the town of East Granby, Connecticut.

The copper mine had been created to provide a source of metal to the town's smiths. It proved difficult to find workers willing to descend the mine's dark, damp interior to obtain the copper, however. After the mine was closed, the Connecticut legislature decided to use it as a prison for criminals, and renamed it Newgate Prison. The first criminal to be sentenced to serve time there arrived in 1773.

At first most of the inmates were Tories, but after the war commenced it became the destination of British prisoners of war. Those incarcerated at Newgate entered the prison through a fifty-foot-deep shaft that led to the underground quarters. The quarters were cold, dark, and dripping with moisture.

After the war Newgate became the first state prison in the United States. It was also used during the Civil War to house Confederate prisoners. Since 1976 it has been a national historic landmark visited by many tourists each year.

Ruins of Newgate Prison in East Granby, Connecticut. Newgate Prison housed Tories and British prisoners of war during the Revolution.

defeated by Washington's army. Just a few weeks later, when the British surrendered to Washington at Yorktown, Virginia, Governor Trumbull celebrated with a jubilant note congratulating the Continental Congress on the war's successful end.

Trumbull's enthusiasm soon turned to less triumphant matters, as Connecticut strove toward rebuilding its society after the war and figuring out how it fit into the newly created United States of America.

Chapter Five

Connecticut After the Revolution

Following the victory of the war, Connecticut, like all the American colonies, struggled to define its economic, social, and political atmosphere. Changes in the way people perceived their role in government contributed to these transformations. Despite opposition by Connecticut's citizens toward a strong central government, the state's delegates to the Constitutional Convention played an important role in preserving the rights of Connecticut citizens while still developing a strong union between the former colonies, now called states.

Postwar Political and Social Changes

By the end of the American Revolutionary War many of the religious and economic disparities in colonial society had disappeared. The citizens of Connecticut had internalized the ideas of individual freedoms embodied in the Declaration of Independence, whereas at the beginning of the war they had been fighting primarily to rid themselves of a "tyrant king." Changes in social and political thought in the new state of Connecticut occurred during the 1780s, as historian Michael Kraus explains:

The war released the energies of vast numbers of people hampered by the discipline of a hierarchical society. They participated more freely in political discussion, and constantly brought pressure on their state legislatures to increase the influence of the mass of men in governmental affairs.[28]

The poor of Connecticut felt justified in expecting the same rights and opportunities that the rich had. All through Connecticut's colonial period the best educated, most prosperous men from the Puritan-Congregationalist Church had traditionally held the positions of leadership. Prior to the war, these men and their families had also held title to great tracts of land, and since voting rights and qualifications to run for office were based on property ownership, this laid the groundwork for a ruling aristocracy.

However, by the time the war was over American society had developed a suspicion for any type of ruling elite and took measures to ensure that no one section of the population could overpower the rights of the others. All over Connecticut, great family estates were broken up due to new laws regarding primogeniture [exclusive right of inheritance by the eldest son], thus abolishing the chance for an aristocracy to flourish and gain control of the government. Moreover, Tory estates were seized and sold off in parcels, offering many people their first chance to own land.

In addition, citizens were motivated by their distrust of a ruling elite to end the old authority of the Puritan-Congregationalist Church. Although in practice this was accomplished gradually over a period of fifty years, the new state government abolished the legality of an established church of the state. The door was now open for people of other faiths to gain leadership positions. As citizens from many religious backgrounds, including Anglican, Methodist, Lutheran, and others, worked with each other in government, their cooperative experiences paved the way for greater religious tolerance in Connecticut.

Religious toleration and freedom brought the issue of slavery into question for many in Connecticut. Slavery had existed in Connecticut since the mid-1600s, although it was not as widely practiced there as in the South. The 1756 census counted 3,019 "Negroes," but not all of them were slaves. Many New Englanders believed the institution of slavery was inconsistent with the freedoms and rights spelled out in the Declaration of Independence, which stated that "all men are created equal." In response to this public sentiment, in 1784 Connecticut enacted state laws that freed all slaves at the age of twenty-five who were born after March 1784. (Complete emancipation in Connecticut did not occur until 1848.)

More citizens than ever before were concerned about how laws and politics affected them in society as a whole; many more were also reading the newspapers and circulars that spread new ideas. As a result, those who could read could more ably participate in government. As the value of literacy was once again touted, the old Puritan value of education flourished in postwar Connecticut as a "crusade against ignorance,"[29] according to Thomas Jefferson. For a few years, schools welcomed many new students, but later as the financial strain from the war became obvious, many schools were forced to close. Even Yale shut its doors for a few years, scattering its students. In spite of these difficulties, most people in Connecticut supported a broad elementary education free to the public. Certain individuals, including Connecticut native Noah Webster, concerned themselves with improving the materials students had to work with. He published children's texts, such as the *American Spelling Book*, which were based heavily on American ideals and traditions. These efforts to educate were motivated by a belief that knowledge was power, thus education was the way to a position of power.

Connecticut native Noah Webster published children's educational books based on American ideals and traditions.

The social upheaval against ignorance was also obvious in the increase in newspapers, libraries, and public lectures. Political literature circulated in the towns and countryside of Connecticut, allowing people to read and form opinions about issues for themselves. This led to a great many public debates between ordinary citizens in town squares, city streets, and backwoods homes.

As the 1780s progressed many of these debates turned to the issue of what kind of government would best serve the needs of the states. Many feared big government, and yet they acknowledged that weak authority, such as that granted to the Continental Congress, was fairly ineffective.

The problem was that during the war Connecticut had willingly set aside its individual interests to unite with the other colonies against a common enemy. Once that enemy was gone, the desire to keep a union with other colonies dissipated. One of the reasons for this attitude was that people in Connecticut tended to be more loyal to their community than to a distant central government. This was directly related to the old Puritan system, where most people participated in local elections and left higher affairs to the authorities. Moreover, people in Connecticut had little in common with the colonies of the South or even the others in the North, many of whom had very different economies, social climates, and political backgrounds. Historian Harry J. Carman explains:

> [The] Patriot forces disagree[d] on the questions of the division of power in the new nation. Small southern frontier farmers wanted stronger national government for protection against the Indians. Some of their counterparts in New England feared that a stronger government would interfere with their local interests. Merchants . . . might resist closer union. . . . Local problems and interests largely determined where a particular group stood on the question of an effective national government.[30]

Connecticut felt that it was doing just fine on its own, operating on a state constitution that strongly resembled its former colonial charter. This constitution included a bill of rights that guaranteed the right to a trial by jury, freedom of the press, and the right to petition. Reflecting suspicion of a central authority, the constitution gave the governor no right to veto the legislature, which held the balance of power. However, the pressures of economic strain were soon to show

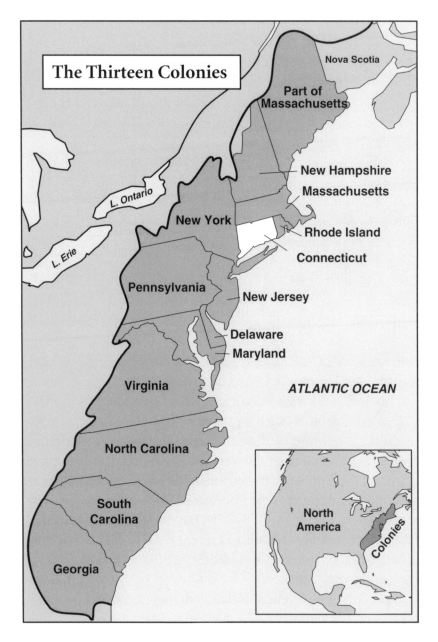

citizens in Connecticut how detrimental the lack of a centralized government could be to the preservation of their liberties.

The Postwar Economy

The war with England had been good for business in Connecticut, and for a few years thereafter, prosperity continued. The large intercolonial and foreign market for food and other goods especially benefited farmers and artisans. Commerce with China, Hawaii, and other regions in the Pacific exploded. Manufacturing, commercial banks, and land companies rose up all over the countryside. However, shipbuilders and privateers, such as those who had lost their entire fortune in the attack on New London, were left destitute after the war.

The high optimism of the times allowed companies to feel secure about extending credit to farmers, merchants, and others. In 1785, however, Connecticut's economy, like that of many other states, fell into a depression resulting from the lack of proper currency and skyrocketing inflation. Farmers found there was no market for their produce and could not pay their property taxes or mortgage interest. Land companies and banks failed to receive payment for credit extended or interest. Many farmers had their property foreclosed. Soldiers returning from the army, which Washington had disbanded in 1783, resorted to selling the wage certificates they had been given for their war service. Often they received only one-eighth of the certificate's former value. The cities of Connecticut were filled with jobless artisans and laborers. Farm wages fell to a low of forty cents a day.

Desperate debtors called for the printing of more currency, but this was no solution because the excessive amounts of colonial currency printed during the war had already rendered it almost worthless. Overwhelmed by debt, many farmers, artisans, laborers, and small shopkeepers were imprisoned, their property seized by tax collectors and creditors. By 1786 the situation was so dire that local courts had enacted laws to prevent creditors from collecting debts. Alarmed, Trumbull and other state officials sought aid from the Continental Congress.

However, the weak central authority the Articles of Confederation granted to the Continental Congress rendered it unable to carry out

Farms that had been prosperous during the Revolutionary War were struck with hard times afterward. As the United States fell into a depression, many farmers, unable to make loan and tax payments, had their property foreclosed.

domestic or foreign policy, and it could not regulate interstate trade. Only the states held the authority to make policies affecting their citizens, and thus the congress could not intervene with a measure such as raising funds by levying a tax.

Debating and Developing the Constitutional Framework

Unable to help the individual legislatures of the states, the Continental Congress realized it needed to throw out the Articles of Confederation and create a new, stronger central government. The question was, What type of government would serve the states' needs best? Many people in Connecticut feared a strong central

"Brother Jonathan" Trumbull

The only governor to remain in office during the Revolutionary War, Jonathan Trumbull played a significant role in Connecticut's participation in the war effort. Born in 1710, Trumbull grew up in Lebanon, Connecticut, where he was trained in the ministry. He attended Harvard, where he earned a master's degree in theology.

Trumbull became a minister, but by 1738 he had taken over the merchant business from his father. He was a major businessman in Lebanon for thirty years. His political career began in 1733 when he was elected to the Connecticut General Court.

When the Stamp Act was passed in 1765, Trumbull became the leading opposition spokesperson for the citizens of Lebanon. According to the Connecticut Society of the Sons of the American Revolution, Trumbull wrote to Governor Fitch: "The People in this part of the Colony, are very jealous of their Liberties; and desire that the most Vigorous exertions be made for the repeal of the Late Act of Parliament which they look on to be utterly subversive of their Rights and Priviledges both by Charter, and as English Men."

When Fitch refused to oppose the act, Trumbull joined the secret society the Sons of Liberty, which spread opposition all over Connecticut. Fitch was voted out of office, with Trumbull elected deputy governor under his fellow Patriot, Governor William Pitkin.

Pitkin died in 1769, elevating Trumbull to the office of governor. He encouraged the citizens of Connecticut to support rebel activities and after the enactment of the Boston Port Bill, he took measures to ensure his own colony would be well stocked with supplies if Connecticut harbors were closed in the future.

When the colonies declared their independence from England, Trumbull was the only governor who supported the act. With the outbreak of war, he authorized the building of gunpowder mills, ironworks, and other munitions factories in Connecticut towns in order to keep the Continental Army supplied. His efforts made such an impact on the survival of the colonial troops that General Washington called him "Brother Jonathan."

Trumbull served as governor until 1784, guiding the colony through the political changes of the immediate postwar years. He retired to his home in Lebanon, where he died in 1785.

government would oppress them and strip them of their freedoms. However, others believed a strong central government was needed in order to protect those individual freedoms. The people who supported a central authority came to be known as Federalists, and their opponents as Anti-Federalists.

Young, ambitious Alexander Hamilton was the Federalist leader, and one of his most ardent supporters was Roger Sherman, who had represented Connecticut in the Continental Congress. When Hamilton raised the idea of forming a Constitutional Convention to develop a stronger central government, Connecticut sent three delegates, including Sherman, Oliver Ellsworth, and William Samuel Johnson, to attend.

During the four summer months that the convention met in 1787, Sherman, Ellsworth, and Johnson argued for a framework of government that would be strong and yet preserve the liberties of the individual states. Sherman in particular was a leader for the smaller states, whose rights he tenaciously guarded against the power and influence of the larger states. He supported measures that strengthened the federal authority, but only when they did not infringe on states' rights. During the convention Sherman remarked that, "Each state, like each individual, had its peculiar habits, usages and manners, which constituted its happiness. It would not therefore give to others a power over this happiness, any more than an individual would do, when he could avoid it."[31]

One subject that the delegates of the Constitutional

Federalist leader Alexander Hamilton supported the idea of a strong, central government.

Convention could not agree on was how to give the individual states fair representation in the federal government. Representation was the medium through which states' rights would be exercised. Without fair representation the rights of some states might be usurped. The larger states argued that with their large populations, they should be entitled to a greater number of representatives. However, the states with smaller populations feared their fewer representatives would be completely overwhelmed by those of the larger states. They argued

At the Constitutional Convention, Connecticut representative Roger Sherman argued against infringement of states' rights by the federal government.

that their citizens deserved an equal amount of representation with larger states. Sherman solved the problem by introducing an idea called the Connecticut Compromise, which was adopted as part of the developing Constitution in July 1787. The compromise provided for the creation of a bicameral legislature comprising a Senate and a House of Representatives. Two senators would represent each state, while each state's population would determine the number of its representatives in the House.

The Fifth State

After the convention completed its work, it presented the new Constitution to the states for ratification. In Connecticut there were fierce debates about whether the state ought to approve the new government framework. It meant submitting to a strong central authority, something people in Connecticut had never done before. Roger Sherman spoke out in support of ratification, explaining how the system of checks and balances would prevent any one branch of the government from overpowering the others. Harry J. Carman explains why the Constitution was finally accepted by independently spirited states, like Connecticut:

> [The framers of the Constitution] discovered a plan that permitted both the federal and state governments to act effectively. At the same time, they were able to overcome the principal deficiency of the Confederation by circumventing the question of how to make a state obey the Federal government. Under the Constitution, the national government operates directly in regard to the individual rather than indirectly through the states. . . . Federal power beyond that of the states was further assured by requiring state officials to take an oath to uphold the federal Constitution.[32]

Assured that states' rights would be protected, the legislature of Connecticut ratified the federal Constitution with a vote of 128 to 40 on January 9, 1788, becoming the fifth state to officially join the United States of America.

Roger Sherman

A signer of both the Declaration of Independence and the U.S. Constitution, Roger Sherman was one of the most influential statesmen to serve Connecticut. Born in New Towne, Massachusetts on April 19, 1721, Sherman was the son of a middle-class farmer and shoemaker. As a child he read avidly in the rare hours between helping his father with the farm and learning the cobbler's trade. He spent little time attending school.

Sherman moved to New Milford, Connecticut, in 1743, where he became a merchant in his brother's business and began to study law. In 1754 Sherman was admitted to the state bar, and the following year he was elected to the Connecticut General Court, where he served for six years. During this time he also served as a justice of the peace and a county judge.

Sherman relocated to New Haven in 1761. In 1766 he was elected an assistant in the Connecticut General Court and also became a superior court judge. During his years in the Connecticut legislature, he gained a reputation for being a shrewd judge of human nature and a man of practical decisions and principles.

By the 1770s Sherman had gained immense respect throughout Connecticut. An early supporter of colonial unity, he was selected to represent Connecticut in the Continental Congress. After the colonies won their independence from England, Sherman served as the mayor of New Haven from 1784 to 1786. He also continued to serve as a member of the Continental Congress, where he was an ardent supporter of creating a stronger central government. He continued to support this position while serving in the Constitutional Convention in 1787. Sherman was instrumental in persuading the Connecticut convention to ratify the new Constitution, making speeches across the countryside explaining how the Constitution would work to protect citizens' rights.

After Connecticut became the fifth state, Sherman served in the U.S. House of Representatives from 1789 to 1791. His final service to the state of Connecticut was as U.S. senator, an office he held from 1791 until his death on July 23, 1793.

As the people of Connecticut entered statehood as part of a greater union, they embarked on a journey of great changes. Connecticut would become a great industrial state, especially in textiles and brass, and it was home to some of the earliest insurance companies that offered policies for fire and life. In addition, Connecticut natives created several inventions, including the steamboat, designed by John Fitch, and the revolver, invented by Samuel Colt. Eli Whitney, who traveled to Georgia, invented the cotton gin, which revolutionized the economy of the South, and he also developed a system of interchangeable parts for muskets.

Connecticut native Eli Whitney developed the cotton gin, an invention that revolutionized the South's economy.

Northern soldiers march during the Civil War. Connecticut's respect for individual and human rights led the state to abolish slavery and fight to preserve the Union during the Civil War.

Many of the transformations Connecticut citizens would see in the future developed from ideas and values that were rooted in their past. The old Puritan value of education and hard work contributed to the existence of people of great intellect and ingenuity in Connecticut society—people who had the knowledge, foresight, and perseverance to create inventions or establish great business enterprises. Likewise, education and the value of individual rights led to a greater understanding of the plight of other human beings. This understanding would eventually abolish slavery in Connecticut and lead its citizens to fight for the preservation of the Union during the Civil War, which was still seventy years in the future. Indeed, the call for freedom, knowledge, and perseverance is still echoed in the rights of Connecticut's citizens and the laws that protect them today.

Notes

Introduction: Connecticut's Legacy

1. Michael Kraus, *The United States to 1865*. Ann Arbor: University of Michigan Press, 1959, p. 48.
2. Quoted in Noel Rae, ed., *Witnessing America*. New York: Penguin Group, 1996, p. 54.

Chapter One: Before the Colony

3. Quoted in John C. Miller, *The Colonial Image*. New York: George Braziller, 1962, p. 240.
4. Quoted in Miller, *The Colonial Image*, pp. 244–45.
5. Quoted in David Hawke, *The Colonial Experience*. New York: Bobbs-Merrill, 1966, p. 157.

Chapter Two: Establishing the Colony for "The Will of the People"

6. Quoted in Kraus, *The United States to 1865*, pp. 61–62.
7. Quoted in Hawke, *The Colonial Experience*, p. 149.
8. Quoted in Hawke, *The Colonial Experience*, p. 149.
9. Quoted in Hawke, *The Colonial Experience*, p. 150.
10. Quoted in "The First Constitution of Connecticut," Connecticut Secretary of State website, 2001. www.sots.state.ct.us/RegisterManual/Section1/firstconst.htm#HISTORICAL.
11. Quoted in Hawke, *The Colonial Experience*, p. 153.
12. Quoted in Kraus, *The United States to 1865*, p. 64.
13. Quoted in Hawke, *The Colonial Experience*, p. 151.
14. Quoted in Hawke, *The Colonial Experience*, p. 171.
15. Quoted in Hawke, *The Colonial Experience*, p. 171.
16. Quoted in Connecticut Secretary of State Website, 2001. www.sots.state.ct.us/RegisterManual/Section1/firstconst.htm#CHARTER.
17. Quoted in Hawke, *The Colonial Experience*, p. 266.

Chapter Three: Daily Life in Connecticut Colony

18. Quoted in Hawke, *The Colonial Experience*, p. 474.
19. Quoted in Kraus, *The United States to 1865*, p. 48.
20. Quoted in Rae, *Witnessing America*, p. 171.
21. Quoted in Rae, *Witnessing America*, pp. 55–56.
22. Quoted in Harry J. Carman, Harold C. Syrett, and Bernard W. Wishy, *A History of the American People: Volume I to 1877*. New York: Alfred A. Knopf, 1960, p. 75.

Chapter Four: Role in the Revolution

23. Quoted in Carman et. al., *A History of the American People*, p. 162.
24. Quoted in "Colonel John Durkee, Norwichtown's Forgotten Hero," The Connecticut Society of the Sons of the American Revolution website, 2001. www.ctssar.org.
25. Quoted in Hawke, *The Colonial Experience*, p. 584.
26. Quoted in "Connecticut's Response to the Lexington Alarm," The Connecticut Society of the Sons of the American Revolution website, 2001. www.ctssar.org.
27. Fort Griswold Home Page, 2001. www.revwar.com/ftgriswold/.

Chapter Five: Connecticut After the Revolution

28. Kraus, *The United States to 1865*, p. 245.
29. Quoted in Kraus, *The United States to 1865*, p. 244.
30. Carman et. al., *A History of the American People*, p. 230.
31. Quoted in Christopher Collier and James L. Collier, *Decision in Philadelphia*. New York: Ballantine Books, 1986, p. 264.
32. Carman et. al., *A History of the American People*, p. 259.

Chronology

1614
Adriaen Block explores the Connecticut River and claims the land for the Dutch.

1633
The Dutch build a trading post—the House of Good Hope—on the site of the future city of Hartford; John Oldham trades along the Connecticut River; the English build a trading post at the site of the future town of Windsor.

1634
Massachusetts emigrants found Wethersfield and settle at Windsor.

1636
Thomas Hooker and followers found Hartford.

1637–1638
Pequot War.

1638
John Davenport establishes the colony of New Haven.

1639
Fundamental Orders of Connecticut adopted by the newly united towns of Hartford, Wethersfield, and Windsor.

1643
Connecticut joins the New England Confederation.

1646
New London founded by John Winthrop Jr.

1662
Governor John Winthrop Jr. obtains a royal charter for Connecticut.

1687
Edmund Andros takes over government of Connecticut; the charter is hidden in the Charter Oak.

1689
Andros is overthrown and Connecticut resumes government under its former charter.

1701
Collegiate School is established by the General Court.

1717
Collegiate School is moved to New Haven and renamed Yale.

1740
Pattison brothers begin tinware manufacture at Berlin.

1755
Connecticut's first newspaper, the *Connecticut Gazette*, is printed in New Haven.

1765
Sons of Liberty founded in response to Stamp Act.

1766
Governor Thomas Fitch is defeated in office by William Pitkin after he refuses to reject the Stamp Act.

1774
Silas Deane, Eliphalet Dyer, and Roger Sherman represent Connecticut as delegates to the First Continental Congress.

1775
Connecticut natives Ethan Allen and Benedict Arnold seize Fort Ticonderoga from the British; first gunpowder mill in Connecticut built at East Hartford.

1776
Samuel Huntington, Roger Sherman, Oliver Wolcott, and William Williams sign the Declaration of Independence as representatives of Connecticut.

1777
British raid and burn Danbury.

1779
British raid New Haven, Fairfield, and Norwalk.

1781
Benedict Arnold leads attack on New London and Fort Griswold.

1784
Jonathan Trumbull retires from Connecticut governorship; Connecticut passes laws providing for the emancipation of slaves born after March 1784 at the age of twenty-five.

1787
Oliver Ellsworth, William Samuel Johnson, and Roger Sherman represent Connecticut at the Constitutional Convention.

1788
Connecticut ratifies U.S. Constitution at Hartford convention.

For Further Reading

Tracy Barrett, *Growing Up in Colonial America.* Brookfield, CT: Millbrook Press, 1995. This book discusses education, training, and leisure activities for children growing up in the American colonies.

Ruth Dean and Melissa Thomson, *Life in the American Colonies.* San Diego, CA: Lucent Books, 1999. This comprehensive book covers topics such as daily life in the cities and rural areas of the colonies, typical employments, immigrants, changes in political, religious, and social attitudes, and relations with the Native Americans.

Dennis B. Fradin and Judith B. Fradin, *Connecticut.* Chicago: Childrens Press, 1994. This book includes a brief section on the exploration and colonial history of Connecticut. It includes a gallery of famous people from the state, a map, and a historical timeline.

Bobbie Kalman, *Colonial Life.* New York: Crabtree, 1992. This book provides brief information and dramatized photographs about colonial homes and towns, family life, play and school for children, men's and women's fashions, travel, and life for a slave family.

Deborah Kent, *America the Beautiful, Connecticut.* Chicago: Childrens Press, 1990. This book offers information on the land, people, and culture of Connecticut. It includes a section with interesting anecdotes on colonial history.

Bonnie L. Lukes, *Colonial America.* San Diego, CA: Lucent Books, 2000. This book offers a comprehensive look at the development of the American colonies. It includes a chapter that covers the settlement and colonial history of Connecticut.

Victoria Sherrow, *Connecticut* (Celebrate the States series). New York: Benchmark Books, 1998. This book provides information about the state's history, geography, government, economy, and people. It includes a section on state firsts and landmarks.

Arthur E. Soderlind, *Colonial Histories: Connecticut.* New York: Thomas Nelson, 1976. This book offers a comprehensive look at the development of religious, social, and political culture in colonial Connecticut.

Charles A. Wills, *A Historical Album of Connecticut.* Brookfield, CT: Millbrook Press, 1995. This book focuses on the state's colonial period and growth and development in the nineteenth and twentieth centuries. It includes a section on famous personalities and a historical timeline.

★ Works Consulted

Books

Harry J. Carman, Harold C. Syrett, and Bernard W. Wishy, *A History of the American People: Volume I to 1877*. New York: Alfred A. Knopf, 1960. This comprehensive text offers in-depth information on the settlement of the colonies, the development of a colonial economy, intercolonial conflicts, and changes in the political and religious climate in colonial culture. It also discusses the process of creating the federal Constitution.

Barbara Clayton and Kathleen Whitley, *Historic Coastal New England*. Old Saybrook, CT: Global Pequot Press, 1992. This book includes brief histories of the coastal towns of Connecticut, including New London and New Haven.

Christopher Collier and James L. Collier, *Decision in Philadelphia*. New York: Ballantine Books, 1986. This book offers an in-depth look at the process by which the Founding Fathers developed the federal Constitution. It provides insight into the motivations of the individual delegates who framed the document, and pieces together how these various factors contributed to the final work.

David Hawke, *The Colonial Experience*. New York: Bobbs-Merrill, 1966. This book provides a comprehensive look at the reasons for colonial settlement, and includes a section devoted to New England history. It also discusses the politics, society, economy, and religion of the colonies.

Paul Johnson, *A History of the American People*. New York: HarperCollins, 1997. This book offers an in-depth look at the early settlement and colonial era of the United States. It includes informative sections on the political impact of the Great Awakening, colonial politics on all levels, and the development of the colonies' independence from England.

Michael Kraus, *The United States to 1865*. Ann Arbor: University of Michigan Press, 1959. This book explores the motivations behind settlement of the colonies, with brief sections devoted to Connecticut, and the political and social changes of the 1700s that led to the war for independence.

John C. Miller, *The Colonial Image*. New York: George Braziller, 1962. This anthology provides a glimpse of colonial life and attitudes through firsthand accounts, essays, and sermons by colonial notables. There are several descriptive sections on the Pequot War and informative writings that reveal Puritan thought.

Noel Rae, ed., *Witnessing America.* New York: Penguin Group, 1996. This anthology includes firsthand accounts from Americans between 1600 and 1900. The topics cover arrivals in America, childhood, marriage, working, housing, food, leisure, religion, crimes, tragedies, and death.

Internet Sources

Colonial Hall website, "Biography of Roger Sherman," 2001. This article offers information on the early life, career development, national contributions, and character of Sherman. www.colonialhall.com/sherman/sherman.asp.

George DeWan, "Nathan Hale: Failed Spy, Superb Patriot," *Long Island Historical Journal.* This interesting article offers a glimpse into Hale's personality and speculates about the true events of his mission, capture, and execution. www.lihistory.com.

Puritan Sermons website, "Thomas Hooker," 2001. This site includes an article on Thomas Hooker that briefly covers his move from Massachusetts to Connecticut and his belief in greater religious and political liberty. www.puritansermons.com/banner/murrray5.htm.

Websites

Connecticut Secretary of State website, 2001. This site offers information on and copies of the text of the Fundamental Orders of Connecticut and the colonial charter. www.sots.state.ct.us.

The Connecticut Society of the Sons of the American Revolution website, 2001. This site offers several articles that discuss Connecticut's role in the Revolutionary War. www.ctssar.org.

Connecticut State website, 2001. This site provides a brief summary of the state's early exploration, settlement, government, and economy. www.state.ct.us.

First Nations website, "Tribal Histories," 2001. This site provides comprehensive articles on the history and culture of the Pequot and Mohegan tribes. www.dickshovel.com.

Fort Griswold Home Page, 2001. This page includes detailed information on the attack of New London and the fort in 1781. www.revwar.com/ftgriswold/.

Old Newgate Prison website, 2001. This site offers brief information on the history of the prison. www.eastgranby.com/historicalsociety/newgateprison2.htm.

Index

Index

Hale, Nathan, 61, 62–63
Hannah (British ship), 64, 65
Hartford
    beginnings of, 11, 13, 26–27
    as center of commerce, 42–43
    Fundamental Orders and, 28
    manufacturing during Revolutionary
        War in, 61
    see also Good Hope, House of
Hartford Courant (newspaper), 50
Holmes, William, 12
Hooker, Thomas
    founding of Hartford by, 26–27
    suffrage and, 25
        Fundamental Orders and, 27–28
hornbooks, 44, 46
houses, 15
Hull, William, 62
Huntington, Sam, 58

Ingersoll, Jared, 54–55
insurance, 81
inventions, 81
ironwork, 41
Iroquois League, 14

James II (king of England), 34, 37
"Jan Kees," 41–42
Jefferson, Thomas
    Declaration of Independence and, 60
    on education, 71
Johnson, Edward, 20–21
Johnson, Stephen, 53–54
Johnson, William Samuel, 77
Judaism, 47

King Philip's War, 31
Kraus, Michael
    on effect of Revolutionary War on
        participation in government, 69–70
    on principles of Puritans, 8–9

landownership
    colonists and, 32, 34
    Mohegan and, 22
    suffrage and, 28, 39
League of Friendship and Amity, 30–32
Ledyard, William, 65–66
legislature, 38–39
literacy
    importance of, 9, 43–44, 71

Livingstone, Robert R., 60
longhouses, 15
Long Island Historical Journal (magazine),
    62–63
Loyalists. *See* Tories
Lutheranism, 70

manufacturing
    growth of, 38, 40–41
    after Revolutionary War, 74
    during Revolutionary War, 61–62, 63,
        76
    shipbuilding, 41, 74
    during statehood, 81
    of wampum, 17
marches, 31
Mason, John, 20
Massachusetts Bay Colony
    Boston Port Bill and, 56–57
    dissension in, 24–25
    French and Indian War and, 53
    New England Federation and, 32
    Puritans from, 12–13
    Sons of Liberty in, 53
Mattabesic
    land of, 13
    Pequot attacks on, 16
    trade with English, 16–17
men, 52
Metacomet (Wampanoag chief King
    Philip), 31
metalwork, 40–41
Methodist, 47, 70
militiamen, 61
Mohegan
    contemporary, 22
    formation of, 18
    King Philip's War and, 31
    loss of land of, 22
    Pequot War and, 20–21, 22, 23
Mourt's Relation (Winslow and Bradford),
    15
Mystic, 21

Narragansett, 14, 22
"Nathan Hale: Failed Spy, Superb Patriot"
    (DeWan), 62–63
Netherlands, 11, 16
New England Federation, 30–32
New England Primer, 46
Newgate Prison, 67

Picture Credits

About the Author

Christina M. Girod received her undergraduate degree from the University of California at Santa Barbara. She worked with speech- and language-impaired students and taught elementary school for six years in Denver, Colorado. She has written scores of short biographies as well as organizational and country profiles for educational multimedia materials. The topics she has covered include both historical and current sketches of politicians, humanitarians, environmentalists, and entertainers. She has also written *Native Americans of the Southeast* (Indigenous Peoples of North America series) and *Matt Damon* (People in the News series) as well as *Down Syndrome* and *Learning Disabilities* (both Diseases and Disorders series) for Lucent Books. Girod lives in Santa Maria, California, with her husband, Jon Pierre, and daughter, Joni.